PROJECT MANAGEMENT THAT WORKS

To Eric!

Thanks!

PROJECT MANAGEMENT THAT WORKS

Real-World Advice on Communicating,
Problem Solving, and Everything Else You Need
to Know to Get the Job Done

RICK A. MORRIS
with **BRETTE McWHORTER SEMBER**

American Management Association
New York • Atlanta • Brussels • Chicago • Mexico City • San Francisco
Shanghai • Tokyo • Toronto • Washington, D.C.

This publication is designed to provide accurate and authoritative information in regard to the subject matter covered. It is sold with the understanding that the publisher is not engaged in rendering legal, accounting, or other professional service. If legal advice or other expert assistance is required, the services of a competent professional person should be sought.

"PMI" and the PMI logo are service and trademarks of the Project Management Institute, Inc. which are registered in the United States of America and other nations; "PMP" and the PMP logo are certification marks of the Project Management Institute, Inc. which are registered in the United States of America and other nations; "PMBOK", "PM Network", and "PMI Today" are trademarks of the Project Management Institute, Inc. which are registered in the United States of America and other nations; ". . . building professionalism in project management . . ." is a trade and service mark of the Project Management Institute, Inc. which is registered in the United States of America and other nations; and the Project Management Journal logo is a trademark of the Project Management Institute, Inc.

PMI did not participate in the development of this publication and has not reviewed the content for accuracy. PMI does not endorse or otherwise sponsor this publication and makes no warranty, guarantee, or representation, expressed or implied, as to its accuracy or content. PMI does not have any financial interest in this publication, and has not contributed any financial resources.

Library of Congress Cataloging-in-Publication Data

Morris, Rick A., 1972–
  Project management that works : real-world advice on communicating, problem solving, and everything else you need to know to get the job done / Rick A. Morris with Brette McWhorter Sember.
    p. cm.
  Includes index.
  ISBN 978-0-8144-0988-6 (hardcover)
  1. Project management. I. Sember, Brette McWhorter, 1968– II. Title.

HD69.P75M6743 2008
658.4'04—dc22

                                        2008011895

Printing Number

10 9 8 7 6 5 4 3 2

To all of the project managers struggling against the odds and trying to make a difference.

CONTENTS

LIST OF TABLES AND FIGURES

ACKNOWLEDGMENTS

This book would not be possible without some key individuals that played a major role in my career development. To Dan Bailey for getting me started and teaching me the fundamentals of project management. To David Yother for giving a kid a chance. To Don Delashaw who helped show me how to enjoy myself and make project management fun. To Cary Blaes who taught me more about management than he truly knows and for being an exemplary leader. To my team at my first PMO: Renee Hyre, Reuben Russell, Courtney Huesman, Karl Cook, Pamela Smith, Pam Maher, Blair Liggins, Marie Todd, Diane Weldon, and Melissa Peterson. You all taught me so much and I was blessed every day that you let me lead you. To Mark Jones and my team at Highmark Technology for allowing me to follow and fulfill my dreams. I thank all of my teams, clients, consultants, and employees over the years. To my daughter Ramsey, son Remo, and, finally, my wife Stephanie—without you, none of this would truly be possible. You told me many years ago to go out and get a real job! Without you, I would not have found my calling.

PROJECT MANAGEMENT THAT WORKS

INTRODUCTION

Welcome to a *Project Management That Works: Real-World Advice on Communicating, Problem Solving, and Everything Else You Need to Know to Get the Job Done.* The growth in project management is undeniable and is one of the fastest-growing occupations in the world. PMI® has seen membership growth of 1,000 percent in the last 10 years, with members in 157 countries. The membership continues to rise at a rate of 30 percent each year. The U.S. Department of Labor predicts explosive growth for the profession through 2014. Because this is such an exploding profession, there is a great need for a guidebook to help both new and experienced project managers improve their skills and procedures. This book is designed to do just that.

Roughly 7 years ago, I was part of one of the worst projects that I have ever encountered. I was always away from my family, was not excited about my job, and depressed. I was questioning whether or not I wanted to remain a project manager or choose another career path. I decided to walk aimlessly throughout a mall while I contemplated my future. I ended up in a bookstore and wandered over to the business section. I picked up a book called *Radical Project Management* by Rob Thomsett. It was a new take on some common project management theories and presented new ways of looking at managing projects. I was so enthralled by the book that I read it cover to cover right there in the store. It made a significant impact on me and how I manage projects. I decided to stay a project manager.

Reflecting on that time, I decided that I wanted to write a book that did more than just discuss proper project management techniques. Really, I wanted to write a book that was a culmination of the lessons learned, frustrations, and events that have been experienced throughout my career. This is that book. There is a significant gap between the principles of project management and the application of project management in many corporate environments. I often compare it to taking a driving test. We were all taught that your hands should be kept at 10 and 2 on the steering wheel, to signal a certain distance from a turn, and how to properly merge. Yet, almost all of us will break many of those rules when we get behind the wheel of a car. Project management is the same way. Trained project managers learn the principles and reasons for running a successful project. However, when it comes to running the project, we tend to selectively decide what we will and will not do.

Corporate culture and what it will mandate as process is another stumbling block in the path of the project manager. The executives will say that they want to have visibility into the enterprise, yet will not support time tracking to the task level. They want to be notified of issues and risks, but will not spend the money on a system that allows single source entry and tracking. The opposite side of the scale is true as well. Corporations can become so process intensive that it prohibits any real work from being completed. This often leads a project manager to experience frustration and apathy.

There are plenty of books on the market that talk about the right way to do things or strategies that take the buy-in from the entire organization. There are even large corporate strategies such as CMMI (Capability Maturity Model Integration) or ISO 9000 (a standard for quality management), designed to offer guidance. However, the implementation of these strategies can sometimes miss the mark. For instance, I was at a company that was becoming ISO 9000 certified very early in my career and I had to attend a training class. The entire point of the training class was to instruct me on how to answer the auditor's questions. The answers were all centered on knowing where to find the processes I was supposed to follow. Essentially, if I could answer that my process is found in that manual over there, I passed. It didn't necessarily check that I was following the process, just that I knew where it was. This of course is not the intent of the ISO 9000 certification. To be fair, the certification is to ensure that consistent processes are being applied. The point is that the company was looking at the certification as a checkmark on their list of accomplishments or to make the company more marketable. They were not interested in truly changing the organization. Many of the books on the market require corporate buy-in or a corporate initiative to make the change.

This book is written for those who want to impact the way *they* manage projects. The overall result could be a change in corporate culture, but even without that level of support, *Project Management That Works* provides successful techniques that can be applied to any environment. These are not high level theories; they are tried and true processes and systems that have worked in a multitude of different cultures and environments. The book is intended for the project manager who wants to follow the principles of project management, but has been unable to bridge the gap between theory and practical application. Be ready to look at information differently; the theories in this book may not be the way that you currently do things today. Hopefully, you are seeking a different way and are ready to open up to a new perspective. Change is hard and some of these concepts are not quick fixes. They take time, diligence, and focus to complete properly. I promise you, though, these systems can and do work. I hope to be able to make the same impact for you that Rob made on me. At the very least, I hope to provide a tool or technique that improves you as a project manager.

At the end of one of my recent presentations, one of the attendees asked if I were able to go back to the start of my career, knowing what I know now, what would I change? The answer is simple. I would change absolutely nothing. The mistakes, stumbles, hard lessons learned, and issues that I have had to deal with on my project management path has made me the project manager that I am today. Each bump, lesson, or issue has taught me something different and provided me with opportunities to grow. Project management is truly a collection of scars. This book is a culmination of what I have learned from my scars.

This book is laid out in a chapter-by-chapter road map to improving project management skills and resolving common project issues. The destination is great project management. Here is how the chapters work together to deliver superior project results:

- **Chapter 1 – Understanding Yourself** – First, find out who you are and how you will react to situations. How will your personality type filter the events around you? You can't manage a project until you can manage yourself.

- **Chapter 2 – Communicating on All Levels** – Be ready to communicate by identifying and investigating the personality types that are on the project team. Communication is the basis to all good project management.

- **Chapter 3 – Be Trustworthy** – Be truthful at all times. Projects are what they are and presenting the entire picture is important. If the project team can't trust what you say, then the rest of the concepts are useless. Laying a basis for trust will allow you to manage a project effectively.

- **Chapter 4 – Turning Around Failing Projects** – Learning how to turn around projects that are in trouble is an essential skill. This chapter shows how to make sure everyone is being heard and learn what has caused projects to fail in the past. Understanding the issues that cause project failure will ensure that new projects can protect from past issues.

- **Chapter 5 – Defining the Word *Done*** – Agreeing on what makes a project or portion of a project complete is another basic of project management. This chapter ensures that everyone is communicating on the same level and understands the vision and direction of the project.

- **Chapter 6 – Application of the Iron Triangle (Triple Constraint)** – Find out what is truly driving the project. Is it cost focused, resource constrained, or driven by a date?

- **Chapter 7 – PERT Methodology in Project Planning** – Estimate the unknown. Get better estimates at the task level to ensure that the total effort is understood.

- **Chapter 8 – Customer Focus Starts with Great Requirements** – Understand the requirements and ensure that the right people are a part of the definition.

- **Chapter 9 – Do Not Sacrifice Your Team at Any Cost!** – Protect the team and keep them out of harm's way. Watch the commitment level and ensure the quality of life.

- **Chapter 10 – Myths About Status Meetings** – Be productive with the project team's time. Run great meetings and make sure that they count.

- **Chapter 11 – Patriots and Scuds** – Avoid the normal meeting tricks and watch for sabotage.

- **Chapter 12 – A Real Risk Assessment** – Make sure that the time spent analyzing risks are productive and that they incorporate lessons learned from previous projects.
- **Chapter 13 – How to Put Risk in a Project Plan** – Protect the contingencies that have been planned into the project. They are for the project manager to manage.
- **Chapter 14 – Data Rules All!** – Bring everything together and present the data of the situation. Data, in the end, trumps all arguments.
- **Chapter 15 – Project Manager: The Strategic Resource** – Understand your role in the enterprise and assist in collecting data, monitor results, and help make key decisions in the enterprise.
- **Chapter 16 – Making Positive Change to Your Corporate Culture** – Utilizing the data slowly removes the emotional conversations from the corporate culture. Successful project management and successful projects leads to a positive change in the corporate culture.

UNDERSTANDING YOURSELF

There are a tremendous amount of business and leadership books on the market. Some of them will have a profound impact on the reader's life, but some can be dangerous as well. For example, a new manager, Keith, brought in a star employee (and current friend) for an impromptu coaching session. Keith had been watching his friend and noting several things in his life. In Keith's observations, he saw the employee start tasks (even personal goals) with great vigor and excitement, but noted he never seemed to follow through. Keith had just finished reading a book on how to motivate employees and was excited to apply what he had just read. He thought that all his staff needed was a conversation to light a fire under him so that he could follow through on the activities he had started. He wanted to discuss the employee's failure to finish projects at home as well as on the job. Keith launched into a monologue about how he had watched the employee start a weight-loss program, brag about how much weight he was losing, yet it looked like he had quit the program. He had also heard the star employee talk about working with a charity, but hadn't heard any updates. Keith announced that he was concerned about the employee and felt he needed to learn how to finish what he had started. The conversation focused only on outside activities, not work-related items.

Later, after thinking about their discussion, the employee marched back into the office and angrily said that Keith didn't know what he was talking about. Yes, the employee had started a weight-loss program, but it required weekly office visits, which the travel requirements for his current position prevented him from attending. He had also started working with a charity, but due to work demands had to leave, but none of that had anything to do with his work. In fact, the new manager didn't mention it at all and just seemed to be complaining about a general failure to finish things. The employee said he was upset at the approach the manager had taken to discuss this, especially because they were also friends. Keith was stunned, but after he thought about the situation, he replied, "I'm sorry. I've been reading a new book on employee motivation, and I guess I didn't apply the concepts very well."

Keith was so eager to apply the points in the book that he failed to take several points into consideration. These issues included understanding why the employee had stopped some of the outside activities, what the current relationship was between the employee and manager, and the fact that his friend had never had a conversation like this with him before. Keith also failed to consider that as a supervisor, it was not appropriate for him to criticize choices in his employee's personal life, even if he thought he was being helpful. He failed to bring the conversation around to any work-related issues.

Another manager, Juanita, went to visit a profound and world-renowned speaker. The advice offered was very straightforward and tough. It was a great approach, however, it was not one that Juanita could see herself using. For instance, when seminar attendees asked how to motivate someone, the speaker would state, "You just tell them to do it. If they don't, you take disciplinary actions." When asked how to deal with unrealistic project completion dates, the speaker said that you just reset them. It was an almost arbitrary or matter-of-fact statement. When Juanita dug into the speaker's theories and background, she realized that he had been a high-level manager at his former company. He had instant authority in his position. Juanita was in an environment where she did not have the same authority. She could not apply his principles because she did not share the same authority level or personality type. She could not employ the "do-it-because-I-said-so" communication type. She had almost no authority at all. She was hoping to learn how to influence teams to perform, not order them around arbitrarily.

These scenarios demonstrate that until you know who you are and how you react to a situation or event, you cannot possibly coach someone else in any effective manner. You are also less likely to craft a proper message that will be meaningful for them. Could the new manager have been more effective had he approached the coaching session with concern versus straight motivation? Can the seminar attendee find the core of the speaker's message and apply it to her environment?

Communications are based on senders and receivers. Each shares responsibility for the communication. Understanding yourself (and your weaknesses) allows you to compose a more complete message by knowing your communication strengths and utilizing them properly.

It has been said many times that people's strengths are also their greatest weaknesses. One manager's strength might be that he can process information quickly in his head. The weakness is that sometimes his mind is processing information before the conversation or event is over, causing him to lose the intensity with which he usually listens, or causing him to miss some key information. Another manager's strengths might be a passion for project management and for life. The resulting weakness might be that he or she can be overexuberant or even quick-tempered. It is important to be able to identify these traits in ourselves so that we can learn to manage them and optimize our skills, while downplaying or compensating for our weaknesses. It is only once we are able to manage ourselves, that we have any hope of effectively managing others.

Great managers take the time to understand how they will react in a situation and are honest in their evaluations so they can then learn to control and mitigate their weaknesses. When something bad happens and a manager with a quick temper can feel and recognize that inner fire in his chest, he can learn to take a deep breath and control his tone of speech. When a manager hears an update and someone is talking, he or she can wait to take notes until after the speaker is finished. Waiting to do this creates a fear that they might forget a point, and makes him or her concentrate harder and listen more intently than if he or she was taking notes throughout the entire discussion.

◼ DISC Profile

The DISC profile was created by William Moulton Marston (Mr. Marston also created the first functional lie detector and the Wonder Woman comics). As the DISC profile has evolved, it has taken on many meanings, but for purposes of this book, we will use Dominant, Influencing, Steadiness, and Conscientious. The profile tests your personality characteristics and places you into one of the categories. Understanding which category you and your employees are in can help you become a better manager (Chapter 2 discusses how to use this profile with your team). Here is a much scaled-down version of this test. For one that's more detailed, you can take a variety online. Whatever you do, take it (Table 1-1).

Please circle the description in each line that best describes you.

TABLE 1-1. DISC PROFILE

Category	1	2	3	4
Behavior pattern	Direct/ controlling	Direct/ supportive	Indirect/ supportive	Indirect/ controlling
Pace	Active/ decisive	Active/ spontaneous	Passive/ relaxed	Passive/ systematic
Inner need for	Power and control	Popularity and acceptance	Sincerity and appreciation	Accuracy and precision
Fears	Being taken advantage of	Loss of social recognition	Sudden changes and instability	Personal criticism of work
Security through	Control and leadership	Playfulness and approval	Friendship and cooperation	Preparation and thoroughness
Motivated by	Results, challenge, action, and the "win"	Recognition, approval, visibility, and the "show"	Relationships, appreciation, the "participation"	Being right, quality, the "process"
Major strength	Goal-oriented, gets things done	Enthusiasm, gets people motivated	Good people skills, team player or leader	Thoroughness, accuracy in analyzing
Major weakness	Can be insensitive to others' feelings	Impulsive; may not focus on details	May sacrifice results for group harmony	Overly cautious; can be too thorough

TABLE 1-1. DISC PROFILE (CONTINUED)

Category	1	2	3	4
Teamwork	Initiates action, takes charge, works toward goals	Influences and motivates people to work together	Builds relation-ships, ensures follow-through, supportive	Focuses on details; offers technical skills and quality control
Time management	Focus: efficient use of time; likes to get to the point	Focus: tends to rush to next exciting thing	Focus: spends time in personal interaction	Focus: works more slowly to ensure accuracy
Decision making	Decisive, at times impulsive, makes decision with goal in mind	Intuitive; quick and spontaneous, lots of wins and losses	Relational, makes decisions more slowly, needs input from others, avoids risks	Reluctant; cautious, logical, thorough, needs lots of data
Communication	One-way; not as good a listener, better at Initiating	Enthusiastic; stimulating, often one-way; inspiring	Two-way flow; a good listener	Good listener, especially in relation to tasks
Conflict style	Autocratic	Attacks	Acquiesces	Avoids
Sensitivity to the feelings of others	Tends to be insensitive; sees life as a battle	More sensitive to others, wants others to be happy, quick to offer support	Conscious of feelings, tries to avoid hurting others, avoids conflict and controversy	Task-oriented, takes a logical approach to feelings
Totals				

Now count the number of answers in each column. Column 1 is D. Column 2 is I. Column 3 is S, and column 4 is C. Whichever column has the highest score is your dominant personality type. There is a brief description of personality types in Table 1-2.

The following sections will help you understand how to use the information the chart has given you.

TABLE 1-2. PERSONALITY TYPES

Category	D	I	S	C
Basic motivation	Challenge and control	Recognition and approval	Stability and support	Quality and correctness
Basic desires	• Freedom from control • Authority • Varied activities • Difficult assignments • Opportunities for advance-ment • Choices, rather than ultimatums	• Prestige • Friendly relationships • Freedom from details • Opportunities to help others • Opportunities to motivate others • Chance to verbalize ideas	• An area of specialization • Identification with a group • Established work patterns • Security of a situation • Consistent, familiar environment	• Clearly defined tasks • Details • Limited risks • Time to think
Responds best to leader who	• Provides direct answers • Sticks to task • Gets to the point • Provides pressure	• Is fair and also a friend • Provides social involvement • Provides recognition of abilities • Offers rewards for risk-taking	• Is relaxed and friendly • Allows time to adjust to changes • Allows to work at own pace • Gives personal support	• Provides reassurance • Listens to suggestions • Spells out detailed operating procedures • Provides resources to do tasks correctly
Needs to learn	• You need people • Relaxation is not a crime • Some controls are needed • Sensitivity to people's feelings is wise • Everyone has a boss	• Time must be managed • Deadlines are important • Being respon-sible is more important than popularity • Listening better will improve one's influence	• Change provides opportunity • Friendship isn't everything • Discipline is good for us • Risk taking is sometimes necessary	• Optimism leads to greater success • Thorough explanation is not everything • Total support is not always possible

TABLE 1-2. PERSONALITY TYPES (CONTINUED)

Category	D	I	S	C
Needs to learn	• Self-control is very important • To focus on finishing well is important			
Perceived strengths	• Independent • Efficient • Practical • Determined	• Enthusiastic • Dramatic • Outgoing • Personable	• Patient • Dependable • Reliable • Agreeable	• Persistent • Organized • Serious • Industrious
Potential weaknesses	• Pushy • Dominating • Insensitive • Unreasonable	• Egotistical • Undisciplined • Manipulative • Talkative	• Awkward • Dependent • Slow • Fearful	• Moody • Indecisive • Moralistic • Picky

▢ Fostering Communication

The information you learned from DISC can help foster the right kind of communication between yourself and your team. It will also help you learn how to craft messages and lead properly. How does knowing the DISC information help you lead more effectively? It starts with honesty. For instance, if you are a high "C," one of your perceived weaknesses is that you can appear moody. If you are honest and look inside yourself, you will recognize the trait. Now that you are equipped with this knowledge, when a situation presents itself and you feel irritated or angry, your first step can be quick analysis. Ask yourself if this is a situation in which it is appropriate to be irritated (or are you feeling irritable and taking the situation out of context?). That simple step, that little realization could prevent you from launching a tirade that will only damage relationships.

▢ Responding to Types

Notice how there are no shared traits between the columns in the entire "Responds best to leader who:" row? If you have a team of high "S's," what would be their reaction if your messages were direct with pressure? Or if you had a team of high "D's" and your messages were friendly or slow to make the point? One leadership type does not fit all. Determine the makeup of your team and then craft the message in the appropriate way that will speak to the individual personalities of your team.

For example, a project manager, Karen, was given an assignment that had been consistently behind schedule and team morale was low. The first thing she did was to perform a DISC profile of the team. Out of ten developers, nine of them were high "D" and only one was a high "S." Referring to the DISC chart, she saw that the dominating drives for the team were "Challenge and control." It was made up of individuals who, according to the profile, enjoyed difficult assignments, could be challenged, but liked the ability to make their own choices. If they did request a decision, however, they preferred a quick and decisive direct answer. Karen then looked at the past project information. She noticed that the communications were very collaborative and that meetings often had little or no agenda and tended to run long. She investigated the issue and risk logs and saw that they were continuing to grow, but very few were closed. When she started to talk to the team, she heard complaints about the former manager being unable to make a decision or being fearful to go out on a limb. Members also complained about what appeared to be a lack of project scheduling. The team often found themselves asking the project manager what to do next.

Armed with this new knowledge and understanding of the team dynamic, Karen put together a three-point plan:

1. She would hold a team meeting regarding the issue log and request that members bring their resolutions. The first meeting would be engineered to close as many issues as possible. The more difficult topics, requiring more analysis, would be assigned to a team member for resolution. Subsequent meetings were scheduled that contained the issues to discuss and the alternative solutions. These were set out in defined agendas with clear objectives for each meeting.
2. She instituted a daily task and progress log. She created an individual to-do list for each team member and requested feedback on what was completed on a daily basis. This list gave each team member a global view of all of his or her tasks.

3. She created a system that challenged the team to resolve out-standing issues, complete tasks, and provide assistance to others. It would reward the behavior that pushed the project to completion. Rewards could be as simple as giving a lunch coupon to the person that resolved the issue or special recognition at a staff meeting. She also instituted a "thank-you" policy that allowed team members to thank others openly in team meetings. This brought positive emotions to the project meetings and built a stronger collective team.

Instituting this plan, Karen found an immediate and beneficial surge of activity. Issues were being resolved, team morale was up, and the project was moving positively again. The key to the turnaround was understanding her team, finding an effective way to communicate with them, and enforcing their basic desires. Because they were high "D's," they wanted challenge and control. They also needed direct and to the point communications.

The previous project manager that was replaced in the above example was a fantastic at her job. She had a great track record and had never really experienced the kind of trouble that she had on this project. However, she didn't know how to adjust her communication styles based on what the team needed to be successful. For a project manager, using one style to manage all projects is no longer useful. To be truly successful, you must adapt the way you communicate to your team's needs.

▨ Working Through Weakness

It is essential that you understand your own weaknesses. If you do not understand how you will react to a situation, then how can you expect to craft the proper message to your team? Once you understand your own weaknesses, you can learn how to work around them or how to improve on those areas. Look at the weaknesses this assessment has revealed about you and your management style and improve them or compensate for them. Take a look at the following examples:

High "D": Understand that sometimes your determined and independent style could appear to be pushy or dominating. You may need to learn to listen to others—and make it obvious that you are doing so.

High "I": Understand that your enthusiasm and outgoing nature can make people think that you are egotistical or manipulative. A little self-deprecation can go a long way.

High "S": Understand that your patient and agreeable nature can give the impression that you are slow and fearful. You may need to make the effort to be bold and decisive some of the time.

High "C": Understand that a persistent and serious approach can push people to think that you are picky or moody. Projecting a positive attitude and learning to lighten up a bit can help.

These are not personality faults; they are *perceived* weaknesses. They too can be controlled with effort. We talked about the manager in the beginning of the chapter whose passion often resulted in the weakness of being quick-tempered. Someone who understands this about himself can easily feel the temper beginning to appear. When it does, he simply has a conversation with himself internally. In a flash of recognition, he is able to calm himself and take a measured response. Prior to attaining the knowledge, his behavior resulted instead in a quick blow-up, a recognized overreaction, and an apology.

There are multitudes of personality tests. Myers-Briggs and DISC have been the de facto standards. Make the time to take them. Be honest in answering the questions and find out who you really are. Some of the results will surprise you. If you take the time to understand yourself, then you have taken the first major step in real-world project management.

COMMUNICATING ON ALL LEVELS

E ffective project management begins with an ego check. You must be prepared to take or give direction at any level of the organization. In every project, there is a primary owner of the project. This person provides the financial backing for the project and sets the initial requirements. This person is the project sponsor. There is no requirement, however, that he or she must be at a certain level of the organization. Your sponsor may not always be an executive. In fact, you may be assigned a new project to examine and procure new waste receptacles. Your sponsor could be the janitor!

Generally, a project manager (PM, as we will refer to him throughout the book) shouldn't even be on an organization chart. If anyone can be a project sponsor or stakeholder, then anyone can give direction on project activities. Essentially, the PM reports to the project sponsor and is accountable to the stakeholders. A stakeholder is anyone who is positively or negatively affected by the project. Therefore, the PM has a dotted-line relationship to all levels of the organization, not just to his or her immediate manager. This means that to be truly effective, a PM must quickly be able to analyze, evaluate, and deliver messages in many ways to ensure the effectiveness of the communications. As a PM, you must be able to communicate at all levels of the organization.

Determining Sponsor Styles

Although anyone can be a project sponsor, for most PMs, the sponsor is an executive in their organization. One of the greatest things about being a PM is the visibility that you can have to upper management. Of course, on the other hand, one of the worst things about being a PM is the visibility that you can have to upper management. If your project sponsor is on the C-level (chief information officer, chief executive officer, chief financial officer) and you run a fantastic project, the direct visibility is priceless. On the other hand, if the project is poorly run and full of mistakes, it could end your career. The most difficult hurdle in working with an executive is determining his or her communication styles. Now, however, you have a new tool at your disposal: the DISC profile (see Chapter 1). Of course, you will not be able to walk up to the chief executive officer and ask him or her to fill out one of the questionnaires; nevertheless, you can observe his or her style. You can ask certain questions that help try to discern his or her type. For instance, consider the following questions.

- A simple question to ask is what type of status report is desired. If a detailed report is required that includes dates, costs, variances, issues, risks, etc., then he or she may be more of a high "C" whose basic desire is detailed reporting. You might be asked for a high-level report that shows overall progress, an indicator that shows the overall project status. This could lead toward more of a high "S" personality type. A high "I" type would rather have a status meeting or a conversation. A high "D" may just want an e-mail blurb.

- Observe style at the kickoff or status meetings. First, is he or she even there? If so, is he or she direct (high "D") or listening and offering reassurance (high "S")? Is the stance more motivational or friendly (high "I") or quiet, relaxed, and observant (high "C")?

- What is your overall opinion of the sponsor? Efficient and practical (high "D") or moody and indecisive (high "C")? Is he or she talkative (high "I") or patient (high "S")?
- When a decision is made, is the sponsor relational (high "S") or reluctant (high "C")? Is he or she decisive or even impulsive (high "D") or more intuitive (high "I")?

The key is to try to look over the profile and help discern which personality type is apparent. This will help you figure out how to craft messages for the sponsor. Be warned not to try to categorize anybody completely! Instead, use this information as a guideline to build your initial communication style as the two of you work together.

Delivering Information

Once you have determined the initial style of communication that will work best, begin to deliver information accordingly. The communications model calls for a sender to encode a message and send it to the receiver. The receiver in turn decodes the message and receives the communication. The model also calls for feedback that allows the sender and receiver to confirm that the message has been both sent and received. In the case of delivering the message, soliciting the feedback is going to be the greatest inclination of whether your chosen communication style will be effective. You must be ready to adapt and change the delivery method of your information should the feedback loop warrant it.

As an example, Chelsea was a PM who was assigned to turn around a failing project. When she arrived on site, the situation was analyzed, ideas were solicited from the team, and corrective actions were put in place. Chelsea was under strict orders from the client to solve the current project issues in 2 weeks or her company would lose the entire contract. The assignment was related to a support project in which the team was to resolve issues reported by the customer. On an average day, more issues were opening than could be resolved, causing a tremendous backlog. Her initial communication style was to prepare a daily report showing the number of issues opened, the number of issues closed, the cause of the issues by category, and a detailed plan to resolve the remaining issues. It was quite detailed and lengthy. After the initial report went out, the sponsor of the project requested a higher-level status report that would not show that level of detail. Chelsea obliged by creating a one-line e-mail chart that would show the high-level information. She solicited feedback from the sponsor again to which he responded, "I don't see it." She took this information to mean that he is not seeing the detail he needs. This occurred three more times when Chelsea changed the report and the sponsor stated, "I don't see it." Finally she asked, "What don't you see?" It turned out that the sponsor could not actually see the message due to the use of a different e-mail program than what the PM was using, so the sponsor was only seeing garbled text. He literally could not see the report.

We will talk more about how Chelsea crafted messages and dealt with the sponsor later in this chapter, but the early portion of the story is to stress the feedback loop of your information that you deliver. Do not assume that the message is being decoded and accepted. You must solicit feedback to understand that the message has been delivered. Do not be afraid to ask qualifying questions such as, "What is this report telling you?" or "Is this report effective in letting you know our progress?" Make sure that you are properly decoding messages as well. If Chelsea had asked, "What don't you see?" earlier, she could have saved iterations of the status reports.

Crafting the Message

Once you have refined your communication style, then you can make sure that you begin to craft a message properly. The following information provides some tips for communicating with different personality types.

High "D"

The high "D" generally stands for *dominant* but can also be described as *direct, demanding,* or *decisive.* For this personality type, make sure you stay on topic. Do not allow yourself to carry on or to make broad statements. Communicating with a high "D" means that you should be to the point and give brief, yet direct messages. A high "D" has a basic desire to see results; therefore, you should craft your messages accordingly. You must make sure that you have the facts to back up any results that you deliver, however. Unwarranted comments or communications that you are unable to back up will frustrate a high "D." Many dominant managers are a successful part of the business community. High "D's" are known for their exceptional handling of obstacles, can provide guidance, and can lead an organization to success. Nevertheless, their directness can push away their employees or trample on an employee's feelings. The high "D" wants direct metrics, factual representations, and brief but results-oriented communications.

HIGH "I"

The high "I" common definition is influence but can also be described as inspiring, impressing, and inducing. The influencer tends to thrive in environments that are favorable and friendly. They like to have more social interaction in their communications. The high "I" type does like detail in their reporting but also relies on social interactions as well. They are generally incentive driven and sometimes would rather discuss an issue than make a quick decision or take action on one. They operate more on instinct and the "feel" of a situation instead of a more focused weighing of the options. They tend to inspire their teams to action instead of directing them. In general, high "I" personality types often find themselves in some sort of sales or sales management position. They are generally positive and very persuasive. They would rather coax you to their side than direct you to make a decision. Make sure you always have some sort of personal interaction when crafting your messages to the high "I." Don't just send an e-mail with boring facts. Follow up with a personal phone call offering to discuss the details if he or she would like. A high "I" can have the tendency to become distracted easily, so make sure you do follow up with that phone call, or you may have to communicate the same information again.

HIGH "S"

The high "S" personality type usually means steadiness but can also be described as submissive, stable, and security oriented. The key to crafting a proper message to a high "S" is to allow for time for him or her to process the information. Create an environment that is friendly, but be patient in waiting for responses. Make sure that the communications are clear and balanced. Confrontational stances will only make the high

"S" uncomfortable and distracted while mentally processing the provided data. One of the dominating characteristics for a high "S" is their desire for a stable and predictable work environment. Generally, high "S" individuals enjoy receiving recognition for loyalty and dependability as well as appreciation for their contributions. When crafting messages for the high "S," make sure that you communicate in a consistent manner. If you have bad news or significant changes, make sure that you craft a message in such a way that it is nonthreatening to the high "S." Next, allow time for him or her to understand and come to a decision or comment. Make sure you protect the high "S's" security and stability within the environment.

HIGH "C"

The high "C" personality type usually stands for *conscientious*. It can also stand for *competent, compliant, cautious*, and *calculating*. The most important factor to remember when communicating with a high "C" personality is that precision will count. Make sure that your communications are accurate and allow little room for interpretation. A high "C" tends to get lost in the details of a report, which can lead to slow or lack of decision making. They tend to control the details and always try to maintain a logical approach to project information. High "C's" like to review recommendations in a logical and systematic manner. They like to create systems and make sure that the standards are followed. When communicating with a high "C," ensure that you request and comply with their reporting recommendations.

▨ Team DISC Profiles

As we said earlier, you are not normally able to walk right up and ask a chief executive officer to take a DISC profile. This is not true when you are managing a team, however. In fact, the DISC profile can be a fun and bonding team exercise. The first time you bring a team together should be at some point in the planning process. Before you begin to identify activities or create the work breakdown structure , administer a quick DISC profile. Take the time to understand the team dynamic, and make sure that you understand the communications needs of your team. Chances are that you will have at least one of every type on a project team due to the nature of projects, however, some functionally organized teams will not. For example, the sales department usually is a grouping of high "I's," so although they may have a minority of team members with other personality types, the communications will still be greatly focused on satisfying the "I" type.

In projects, however, you may have equal distributions of types. Imagine a software development company that has a large project to launch a new product. To be truly successful, the team will need a combination of all of the personality types. A high "D" could set the direction of the product, while the high "I's" find a way to market and sell it. The high "S's" and "C's" can create, test, and ensure the quality of the product. Together, they can create a unique product, sell it, and ensure customer satisfaction. The key is that each personality type is valuable to a team and has a role in a project.

After you complete the assessment of the team, the results could lead you to shift, replace, or increase resources depending on the results. If the key is balance, then make sure that you do not have an overwhelming majority of one personality type. There are types of projects when an overwhelming majority is acceptable, but that is a rare occasion. If you understand the personality types and the makeup of your team, then you can ensure that you are communicating with enough variety to guarantee the proper decoding of your messages.

Adjusting the Message

Learning how to adjust your message takes skill and practice and depends on learning how to identify and classify personality types. Great PMs can pick up the tendencies of their sponsors or customers and quickly adjust their message to elicit the response that they desire. Earlier in this chapter, we talked about the PM Chelsea who was assigned to a stressful project that was in need of a turnaround in 2 weeks. The project did not have a PM in the beginning, and now it seemed that there were more issues than the project team could deal with. The company decided they needed to bring in a PM to analyze the situation, create a plan that could appease the client, and implement the plan. The client demanded changes within 2 weeks. The initial meeting with the project sponsor was a disaster. This is an actual story from a PM's experience:

CHELSEA (PM): "Good morning, it is nice to…"

SPONSOR (SPN): (Interrupts) "I don't care what your name is or where you are from; your company is not performing, and I'm sick of it. Identify the issue or your company is out of here."

PM: "OK. We'll start our analysis and get back to you as quickly as possible."

SPN: "Two weeks. We will see then. Now, if you don't mind, I have other matters to attend to."

Needless to say, Chelsea was quite distraught. What did she learn from this initial encounter? First, the sponsor was not very personable and gave direct and decisive commands. There was also a direct threat. Although it was a generalization, she could ascertain that she wasn't dealing with a high "I" or a high "S." Both of those types really enjoy the personal side of communications. They tend to want to socialize first before getting to business. This sponsor was completely about business. A high "C" can have the tendency to share risks or responsibilities, and they ultimately strive for consensus. Therefore, Chelsea decided she was dealing with a high "D" personality. She understood that a high "D" ultimately thrives on the power and authority aspect of being a manager. They like to take risks, make decisions, and dominate their environment. This also means that they hate to be wrong and their egos can be sensitive.

Chelsea worked with the team, and they quickly found the issue. As it turns out, the support issues were being created due to a change in the technology initiated by the customer. Chelsea's organization was supporting an application that utilized a current version of mail software. The client upgraded the mail software without proper notification to Chelsea's organization. According to the contract, if the customer changed the technology, then Chelsea's organization would have an opportunity to test and certify the new application. The change occurred without certification, but because the support organization did not have a PM on the project originally, the proper change control procedures were not followed. This was the root cause of the support issues.

Chelsea still had the problem of more issues opening than could be closed, and now the root cause of the issues had been identified. She immediately put plans in place that would stop the incoming calls for identified issues, repair the environment change, and close out the backlog of support calls. At this point, she had to be careful about how to craft the message back to the sponsor. Every part of her wanted to run into the office, announce how wrongly her company had been treated, and point out that it was his company that caused the problem. This may have felt good to her, but it would not have accomplished anything other than satisfying her ego. Following her deduction that the sponsor was a high "D," she crafted her response and went to visit him.

PM: "I want to report that the issue has been identified, plans are being executed as we speak that will stop the incoming calls, and we are closing out the backlog of open issues."

SPN: "Good to hear."

PM: "We will not need the full 2 weeks to resolve the issue. We appreciate your understanding in this matter."

SPN: "Hopefully you have taken measures to ensure this never happens again."

PM: "We have, sir."

SPN: "Is that all?"

PM: "Yes, sir."

As she was leaving, she stopped and said one more thing.

PM: "One more thing, sir, our contract states that before any new technology is deployed in the environment that can affect our product, it must be certified by us. We are sure that we tested and certified it, but we don't actually have a copy of the test results. Because I have just been assigned to this project, could you forward a copy to me? A formality, really. Have a great day and thank you again."

SPN: "We will get it to you right away."

The best part about this story is as soon as Chelsea said that, she could see the flash of recognition in the sponsor's eye. He wasn't aware that the issue had been on his company's side. She was also pretty certain that he decoded her message. She was fairly certain that he understood that the certification document didn't exist because they did not ask for certification before deploying, thus causing the issues. This story is a great example of crafting a message to a sponsor or executive by using what you can learn about personality types and adapting your message to fit them. If Chelsea had gone into the office and accused, blamed, or acted indignant, the end result would have been the same as if she had never found the problem at all. Instead, she carefully crafted a message that allowed the sponsor to maintain his authority and kept intact his basic desires. The end result? The sponsor signed a new 2-year deal and expanded the scope of the support project.

Proper Communications Management

Communications management can be greatly misunderstood. Many PMs assume that a communications plan is a long drawn-out document. In actuality, it can be administered quite easily using nothing more than a spreadsheet. The key to great communications is to make sure that the pertinent information is given to the team members in a timely manner. There should be a minimum of five items that are communicated to a team on a weekly basis.

1. **Issues:** At a minimum, the next 2 weeks worth of issues should be communicated. It is up to the PM's discretion how many issues to show after the 2 weeks, but showing all open issues is the preferred method.

2. **Risks:** There are many different types of risks. There are some that the PM may or may not want to communicate to the whole team. Which risks are shared with the team is ultimately up to the PM's discretion, however, severe risks should not be withheld from the team unless they could disrupt or damage the team unity. Risks are scored a number of different ways. The most common way is impact (usually a cost or dollar amount) multiplied by probability (the percentage chance that it will occur.) Some systems use a weighted system such as 0 through 3 for impact and probability (i.e., high impact = 3, high probability = 3, risk score = 9). For example, a PM may open a risk because he or she feels that the materials necessary for the project may not arrive on time. He ranks the probability of this occurring as medium (2) and the impact on the project as high (3). His risk score would be 6 (2 × 3). Risk scoring allows the PM to rank the risks so that the PM can prioritize the list of risks. The PM should revisit each risk and risk score

on a weekly basis. The risk scores are expected to change from week to week as new information about the risk is revealed.

3. **Deliverables:** When an item is needed that does not appear on the project plan, issues, or risks, deliverables can be used. A *deliverable* is an item or activity that is not large enough to be on a project plan, consists of an issue or risk, yet still needs to be completed. For instance, "Joey needs to bring 12 copies of the user manual to the next meeting" is a deliverable. It is up to the PM's discretion to choose what is tracked or shown in this section.

4. **Completed Items:** It is good practice to share with the team all of the completed tasks, issues, or deliverables from the previous week. This will allow for input on the validity of the completed items as well as share with the team what work was done. It also prevents having to go around the room to discuss completed items.

5. **Upcoming Tasks (2 weeks):** In this section, the PM lists the tasks from the project plan that are to be started or completed within the next 2 weeks. This is an important step from an awareness viewpoint and is a concise way to notify the team about upcoming tasks. Additionally, it creates awareness for the PM to understand what is expected to be complete in the next 2 weeks.

▨ Communications Documents

At the beginning of each project, the PM should meet with the team to discuss the method and frequency of communicating the pertinent information. There are several document types that should be utilized throughout the project. Each project can vary in the use of documentation and communication methods. Following is a list of the common uses for each document.

STATUS REPORTS

Audience: Sponsors, stakeholders, project team
Frequency: Weekly
Timing: Same time each week (typically on Friday)

Purpose: Communicate weekly progress of project

Description: The status report is a snapshot of the project's progress for the prior week. It communicates the issues, risks, deliverables, completed items, and upcoming project tasks. It is intended to show weekly progress, as well as act as a vehicle to bring the core issues of the project to the forefront. All of the weekly communication expectations can be handled within the status report.

MEETING NOTES

Audience: Absent team members, project team

Frequency: As needed

Timing: As soon as possible after the meeting

Purpose: Documentation of what occurred in the meeting

Description: Meeting notes are intended to be a snapshot of what occurred in the meeting. They convey what decisions were made and document the discussions that take place. The main audience for this document is the team members that were unable to attend the meeting. Additionally, a historical record is created for reference. Some meetings require formal minutes, but this will depend on the type of project. In most cases, a synopsis will suffice.

MEETING AGENDAS

Audience: Project team

Frequency: As needed

Timing: One to 2 days before the meeting

Purpose: Prepare team members for which topics will be discussed in the meeting

Description: Agendas are intended to establish the meeting flow and ensure that all items pertinent to the project are discussed. The agenda should give the attendees ample notice of the expected update items and allow them to prepare their responses.

ISSUES, RISKS, AND DELIVERABLES LOG

Audience: Entire project team

Frequency: Weekly

Timing: As soon as possible after the weekly status meeting

Purpose: Communicate action items and issues

Description: Issues, risks, and deliverables logs can serve multiple purposes. These are itemized lists that require the PM's attention. They can help prioritize tasks and help communicate to the team the items' impact. Logs are not a required communication but are the most effective means of quickly updating statuses received in a weekly status meeting and communicating to the team what needs to be done.

PROJECT PLAN

Audience: Project team

Frequency: Weekly

Timing: Normally sent at the time the status report is sent

Purpose: Show current time frames and tasks

Description: Some team members and sponsors like to see the project plan. It is good practice to make it available to the team upon request or based on the communication plan.

TO-DO LISTS

Audience: Project team

Frequency: Weekly

Timing: Normally sent at the time the status report is sent

Purpose: Itemized list specifically for each resource

Description: It is good practice to send out the to-do lists to the project team members. This is an effective way to communicate what each resource will need to complete for the project. Many project team members dislike the project plan because it can be difficult to understand and the information is not concise. The project plan lists all tasks for all resources. A to-do list contains the specific tasks for each individual resource. The list provides a focused view for each team member of what he or she is supposed to accomplish and when.

BUDGET

> **Audience:** Project sponsor
> **Frequency:** Weekly/monthly
> **Timing:** As needed
> **Purpose:** Communicate the financial status of the project
> **Description:** Depending on the project, the PM may need to keep the financial records of the project.

COMMUNICATION PLAN ADMINISTRATION

The following steps should occur on each project to determine the communication plan:

- Identify the project team.
- Identify the types of documents that the project requires.
- Identify the target day for each document.
- Create a draft communication plan.
- Provide examples of each type of document and ask which documents the team wishes to receive and how often they wish to receive them.
- Document the responses on the communication plan.
- Execute the communication plan.

Proper use of the communication plan should eliminate issues with overcommunicating and undercommunicating with your teams. A sample schedule is provided:

- Wednesday: Status meeting
- Thursday: Updated issues, risks, and deliverables log
- Friday: Meeting notes, status report, to-do lists, budget
- Monday: Weekly status meeting agenda

The key to effective communications is timing. Issues and risks that are pertinent to a project's success should be communicated as quickly as possible. Allowing your audience to decide the way in which they wish to be communicated with is an important step for team building. For example, some team members like to see all project documents. Some team members may only want to see the project status report and not all of the other documents. Taking the time to show the team that you understand how busy they are and that you want to make sure you are communicating the right amount of information at the right time is a powerful way to show the team members that you care.

BE TRUSTWORTHY

To be a great project manager (PM), your team, stakeholders, sponsors, and peers must be able to rely on you. Trust is not given right away; it is earned. Unfortunately, the corporate world has taught many team members to not always be truthful. For instance, an executive may approach a team member in passing and discuss a task. At the end, he may ask, "Hypothetically, how long would this take?" The team member answers, "About 2 weeks." Two days later, the team member finds out that he has been committed to completing the task in 2 weeks. At some point, the "hypothetical" became the actual. This is a standard problem for many people. The next time the team member is asked, he will be much more guarded with their response.

As situations like the one above transpire, teams learn not to trust management. They begin to pad their estimates to make sure that they are not painted into a corner. Then, the PM, wanting to account for risk, will pad the padded estimates given by the team and further inflate the estimate. By the time the sponsor sees it, the estimate is unrealistic from her standpoint. This mistrust leads to the sponsor cutting the estimate by an arbitrary figure, such as ten percent. The next estimate from the PM will then try to account for the 10 percent that the sponsor cut, and a vicious cycle occurs. The team members don't trust management so they pad the estimate. The PM doesn't trust the sponsor, so he pads the estimate. The sponsor cuts the estimate in an effort to try to control costs, and the cycle continues.

This whole cycle is built on missing information. When supplied with an estimate from the team, the PM assumes that this is an estimate that has not accounted for risk. When the sponsor sees it, there is an assumption that padding is built in. Why are these assumptions made? For the most part, the cycle exists because the PM is padding because the team hasn't accounted for risk. It becomes common practice to assume what the other person is thinking.

How is it possible to break this practice? First, make sure you validate your assumptions by asking all of the necessary questions, communicate properly with the team and stakeholders, and tell the truth, even to a fault. This chapter explains how to take the right steps in ensuring that the information provided is always trustworthy.

■ Coping with Questions

Chris was an eager young man who was an on-site PM for a company. He reported to his supervisor and a sales VP. His supervisor managed his day-to-day activities while the sales VP was responsible for the client's overall satisfaction. His supervisor came in one day and asked Chris, "How's everything going?" Chris answered, "Everything's fine." The supervisor then went to a meeting about the project. When the supervisor returned, he was furious at Chris. "I thought you said everything was fine!" he shouted. Chris was aghast. "Everything is fine!" he said. The supervisor asked, "How can everything be fine when I just heard about four issues in a team meeting?" Chris thought about that. There were indeed four issues on the project, but he felt in full control of them. Therefore, he didn't disclose them to the supervisor. The supervisor and Chris then discussed the four issues at length until the supervisor was pacified.

The next day, the sales VP came in and asked, "How is everything going?" Remembering the run in with the supervisor, Chris said, "Well, there are four issues that we are dealing with right now." The sales VP said, "OK," and left. Ten minutes later, Chris was called into a meeting room where the sales VP told the supervisor that she was concerned because there were four issues on the project, and it didn't seem that the PM had them handled. Chris stated, "I do have them handled. You asked how things were going; I told you there were four issues." The sales VP said, "Right, and I expect you to be on top of the issues." The supervisor said, "Chris was on top of the issues, but it appears that we have a communication breakdown."

Obviously, Chris was quite confused. He answered the question he was asked, and it got him in trouble both times. When he tried to adjust his message between the first and second encounters, he still got in trouble. How can he avoid these uncomfortable encounters in the future?

The answer is to qualify the questions.

Qualifying the Question

Qualifying the question means asking more questions to help determine the level of detail that the stakeholder needs. What you're really doing is finding out what the stakeholder truly wants to know. For instance, when the functional manager asks the PM, "How's everything going?" The PM can counter with the following questions: Would you like to know all of the issues that have occurred, or do you want to just discuss the ones that we don't have resolution to?

That simple question can qualify what the supervisor really means. Originally, the supervisor was upset because Chris answered his question of how everything was with a response that everything was fine. There were two major assumptions:

1. Chris assumed that the supervisor wanted to hear issues that should be escalated or issues that did not have active fixes in the works, and so he stated that there were none.
2. The supervisor, on hearing that everything was fine, assumed that there were no issues on the project at all, resolved or otherwise.

Likewise, the supervisor could have asked a follow-up question such as, "So that means all issues are closed?" to qualify the response he received from the PM. This would have eliminated the assumptions. When the sales VP asked, "How's everything going?" Chris' response with detail also caused problems, and he could have qualified that question by asking, "Would you like to know the specific issues or just that we are on top of all of them?"

The sales VP became concerned when she heard a list of issues with no resolution. The two assumptions made in this conversation were:

1. Chris assumed that the sales VP wanted to hear all of the details of the issues.
2. The sales VP assumed that due to the amount of issues and the fact that no resolutions were offered, the PM was not doing his job.

Again, a simple qualification of the question can take away many of the misconceptions. In qualifying the question, it is possible to garner a better understanding of the information being requested so that the answer makes sense and offers the proper amount of information to the questioner.

▧ Don't Lie!

The question has been asked and qualified; now it is time for the proper response. For many PMs, saying that the project is over budget, behind schedule, or just generally in trouble is a difficult task. It is easier to come up with another reason that allows you to blame the situation on someone else. People tend to withhold the real reasons for problems because it makes them feel inadequate or as if they are not performing their job duties well. The fact is, stating that you are ahead or behind schedule, under or over budget, or on or off track is your duty as the PM. Do not be afraid. Honesty is the best policy when it comes to project management. Taking the attitude of "it is what it is" will pay large dividends in the long run.

The obligation of the PM is threefold:

- Assess the current direction of the project.
- Forecast where the project is likely to end up.
- Report the findings to the entire project team.

The reality is that when a project is going badly, PMs often think that this is a reflection of their personal worth versus that of project performance. Instead of notifying the proper people, they begin to pray that the project will turn around. Generally, the project continues on the same path or gets worse. At this point, no amount of praying is going to bring the project back in line. Because of the misguided hopefulness that the project will magically right itself, however, a tremendous amount of time has been wasted, be it 1 week, 1 month, one quarter, or even a whole year! In the meantime, the PM is essentially "doctoring" the project reports or at least telling half-truths in project status meetings. Eventually, the truth will come out. What is the PM supposed to do then? Any amount of explanation will sound like lame excuses, and the trust level with the project team and sponsors is completely blown. Many PMs have lost their jobs due to a failure to be truthful.

Despite these serious consequences, it is not easy to admit that the project is off track or has blown its budget. If it were easy, then anybody could do project management! The reality is that it is hard, but you must set aside your fears and forge ahead.

Dealing with Fear

It is easy to say that you will always tell the truth in project reporting. It is quite another to sit in front of an executive in your organization and state that the project is off track. Most PMs are afraid to do this. How do you deal with this fear? The fear generally centers on disappointing the executive or admitting that the project has not been managed appropriately (which is admitting personal failure). The reality is that people are more afraid of the unknown. They are afraid of all of the potential reactions. To quell your fears, bring options for solutions to the meeting. This places you in control of the situation. You know exactly how the meeting will go: you will explain the situation, offer solutions, and then ask the client how he wants to proceed. You are the one leading the meeting.

When a project is off track, this is usually because it is behind schedule or over budget. The PM's role is not to simply report this as a status, but to present options to repair this. Don't just walk into a status meeting and announce that the project is over budget. Come into the meeting and state that following the current trend, the project is projected to be over budget. Also explain that if we change this or remove that requirement, we can stay under budget. If options are presented, the sponsor is likely to make a decision and move on. If no options are presented, then the sponsor is likely to berate the PM with question after question until he or she understands the situation. If you offer solutions, you present yourself as a professional who is in charge of the project. If you walk in with no solutions, you appear overwhelmed. When you present possible solutions, you divert the executive's attention away from your own performance to the options you have presented. Throughout this book, we present several methods for generating options to present. For this section, know that your role is to present the possible solutions to the issue, as well as presenting the issue itself.

You can also control fear by being confident in the options that you present to the sponsor. If you have to walk into a sponsor's office and state, "The project is behind schedule by 2 weeks," that can be a fearful conversation. Walking into that same office and saying, "The project is expected to be 2 weeks behind schedule; however, if we add a resource to this task, we may be able to make up that time. The best resource would be to add Tom to the team, and he is readily available." This statement offers a solution. Knowing you have a confident attitude for the issue at hand can help you be more positive in the way you handle the conversation. If you present the possible solution and say, "Well, I suppose we could do X or Y, but I don't really know," you do not appear to be confident and in charge. If, however, you go into the conversation and take the approach given earlier in this paragraph, you present yourself as confident and calm.

Admitting You Are Wrong

There are times when the project is off track and it is the PM's fault. This could be due to inadequate planning or a scheduling oversight. The Project Management Institute (PMI®, as we will refer to it throughout the book) believes that an unrealistic schedule or budget is a direct result of poor project management. When it is off track, honesty is still always the best policy. In fact, honesty can save the relationship with the client. Take a look at the following example:

Ryan was the PM running a time-sensitive project. The customer was a servicing company who had roughly 80 people relying on a successful completion. The project had many obstacles. The customer's team and Ryan's team, however, were working quite well together. The only true issue was the lack of consistency in the technology architect role. In general, high-level positions such as that of a software architect, PM, or key subject-matter expert should not change throughout the project. Due to scheduling conflicts, one architect started the project and had to leave midway through the project. The other architect was to come in and deliver the vision. The key discrepancy was that the first architect had a far more advanced knowledge of the end product than the second. Although the knowledge gap was an issue, it did not spell the doom of the project.

The big bang came when the architect discovered that the planned approach was not going to work. The customer, due to time constraints, wanted to use the core product and did not want to have to customize or adjust any of the components. The product had a key flaw that would not fit the overall planned use. Therefore, the team would have to code elements from scratch instead of using the existing code. When the architect presented the problem to Ryan, the team was roughly 3 weeks away from the agreed-upon delivery date to the client. When asked what sort of delay the issue uncovered would cause, the answer was roughly an additional 8 weeks to complete the project. Ryan was aghast, however, there were four choices:

1. Do not tell the customer right away. Come up with many options and hope that some of them will bring the project in line.
2. Covertly degrade the quality of the product so that delivery times could be met, but some of the other functionality could be implemented later.
3. Do not tell the customer and add resources to try to shorten the time frame. Essentially, pray that the date will be met by throwing more resources to the project.
4. Tell the customer immediately and let him or her form options as your team decides what their suggested course of action is and meet later to discuss all options.

Although it seems like this would be a difficult choice, there is only one clear and direct answer. The answer is choice number four. We stated earlier that broaching the subject with the client is easier if options as well as the issue were presented. In this case, time was of the essence, and the PM had to keep in mind that his client had 80 others relying on him.

Choices one, two, and three are common choices for PMs. The motivation for these options is either fear to tell the truth or fear of admitting they are wrong. All three choices mean keeping the customer in the dark until it is too late, which is the worst option possible. Not telling the customer handcuffs him or her from any opportunity to assist or alleviate the time constraint. Choice two is the worst of the four because it is essentially a lie on top of the lie. The customer is not informed and he or she is getting less than what has been paid for while you hope that he or she will not notice.

Ryan, the PM in the current example, chose number four and had a very tough, yet honest conversation with the customer. He informed the customer of the missed technology and that at this time, his team was developing options to rectify the issue in the timeliest manner. He also let the customer know that he was informing him as soon as he found out so that the customer could assist with or develop another option, even if it meant using yet another partner. When the customer asked, "What are your plans to fix this? Can it be done in 3 weeks?" Again, Ryan answered honestly. "To be honest, I don't know what our plans are to fix this. We are looking in to all options to find the best path available, however, it is very likely going to take longer than 3 weeks. It's more likely that it could take 8 to 12 weeks to complete. We hope to have a list of options to you by the end of the business day today. We understand if you need to develop options outside of us, but we would very much like you or your team to be involved in developing the possibilities with us so that we can ensure we are balancing all of your business needs."

When PMs are behind schedule, the normal behavior is to quote the most optimistic delay time possible, to try to reduce the impact of being behind schedule. If this is the approach, you will most likely disappoint the client again. In Ryan's case, it was stated that there would be an 8-week delay, and he accounted for risk by adding another 4 weeks.

In the end, the client invested more internal resources to the project, reduced the scope of the project, and extended the end date by 8 weeks. The project was completed 3 weeks late for a total of 6 weeks from the date the issue was identified. The client, although unhappy that the project was late, decided to do more business with the company and became a personal reference for Ryan. Why? Because they proved they were trustworthy. All projects have issues. An overwhelming majority of projects fail. Knowing these circumstances, who would you rather do business with? The company that doesn't tell you when things go wrong, keeps you in the dark, and covertly degrades quality? Or would you rather do business with someone who notifies you when things are off track, asks for input to the resolution, and is trustworthy?

Use these tips to remain trustworthy in a precarious situation:

- Make sure that the actual error is disclosed. Do not use fancy language or try to softly reveal the issue. Be clear and concise. "There is an issue, and it will affect the project."
- Do not offer excuses. Offer explanations or rationale to the client, but only as a means to explain the overall situation. Start the conversation with a disclaimer to ensure that the client or sponsor knows that it is not an excuse. "I am not offering excuses, but as an explanation, we did not clearly understand the requirement."
- Stay humble. Do not get defensive. People react to bad news in a variety of ways. Anger, frustration, apathy, accusatory statements, and bewilderment are likely results of the conversations. Allow the client or sponsor to work through the shock and calm down. Defensive behavior generally escalates the anxiety, resulting in a straining of the relationship.
- Deal with facts. Do not create hypotheses as to why the project is off track. State only the facts. When anything but a fact is offered, it could come back as an attempt to cover up or place blame. The point of having the conversation is to avoid those feelings by the client or sponsor.

Admitting that the team or the PM made a mistake, caused a delay, or otherwise was wrong in a situation is one of the most difficult things to do. It is almost against human nature to admit fault. As difficult as it may be, it is an extremely important step in becoming a great PM. It doesn't matter how well a project is planned or how detailed the requirements are—a project will have issues. A PM must be prepared to effectively deal with the issues in order to ensure success.

How to Fix Things If You Haven't Told the Truth

There are times when it is difficult to remain honest with a client. Whatever the circumstances, the PM may feel it would be better to not reveal all of the information or not tell the complete truth. Inevitably, however, the truth will come out. Oftentimes, PMs will think that it is their burden to bear when a project is off track. They may withhold information and try to fix it themselves. What they forget is that it is not always their job to fix it! The client must be involved in the tradeoff decisions that come with bringing a project back into compliance. There are some simple steps to follow when a client finds out that the truth has not been told.

- First and foremost, apologize in a sincere way.
- Come completely clean with the client or sponsor. Tell the entire truth, including why you chose to withhold the information. Offer this not as an excuse, but as an explanation.
- Acknowledge that you may have lost the client's trust and you will do whatever it takes to regain the trust through action, not empty promises.
- After the acknowledgment, be quiet and listen. Give the client or sponsor time to process the information and look to them for the instructions on how to proceed.

There may have been a perfectly valid reason to withhold information or to not to tell the truth—or at least at the time you thought there was a good reason. In the unfortunate circumstance when you have not completely told the truth, be prepared for the fallout. Any time integrity, honor, or morals are called into question, it can be difficult to deal with. Keep in mind that you created the situation, however, and you must resolve it.

A PM's role is to bring chaos to order, blurred vision to clear reality, and disorganization to harmony. It is a PM's role to plan, execute, validate, and complete projects. This responsibility includes reporting progress. Many PMs will be tempted to not tell the truth if the project is slightly behind schedule or slightly over budget. They begin to hope that it will turn around. Instead, *slightly* behind becomes *greatly* behind, and a small issue grows into a large issue. To avoid this, a good

PM reports the exact progress. The moment a project goes off track, the PM should ensure that everyone is aware that it is off track and understands what needs to be accomplished to get back on track. This has to be carried out with action and communications, not hope and prayer.

Sometimes It Can't Be Fixed

A program manager (a PM that is in charge of a group of interrelated projects) named Rita was on a client site for 3 years. Rita had become quite close with many people on-site. The contract was ready for re-negotiation. In the meantime, Rita had become ready to move on with her career, but the company did not want to promote her because of her relationship with the client. This issue forced Rita to make a very tough decision about her career. One Monday, she presented her management with her 2-week notice. They seemed shocked but eventually understood that she was going to move on. Due to the contract negotiations, her company asked her not to say anything to the client until they had a chance to formulate a response. She agreed. One full week went by, and the client had not been apprised of the situation. She was getting several requests for future meetings and future commitments that she was reluctantly agreeing to, but Rita felt that she was not being honest. She continued to press her company and notify them that she was being asked for these commitments and was uncomfortable lying. The company continued to ask for her patience and promised that they would reveal her planned departure soon.

During this time, a job fair was underway. One of the senior managers of the client visited the job fair and struck up a conversation with one of the companies' representatives. The person that he spoke with happened to be employed by the company that was hiring Rita. In passing, the person representing the new company said, "Do you know this person? She's coming to work for me on Monday." On Wednesday of the last week for Rita in her old job, there was a standard management meeting that consisted of 30 of the primary decision makers for the client. At this time, the senior official announced to Rita in an open forum, "So, I hear you're starting a new job on Monday." The room fell silent and all eyes were on Rita. She had to admit that she was leaving. Obviously, quite a few people were upset.

A representative from the client called the company's management in and announced their displeasure. As is the case in most of these kinds of misunderstandings, the company was scared to lose the account, so they created more fabrications as to why Rita was leaving and why they hadn't informed representatives of the client. It became a very ugly situation. When it was over, the company and the client reconciled, but Rita's reputation was tarnished, and a 3-year career and bonding experience was diminished.

This is a true story, and the unfortunate part is that it happens quite often. In many cases in projects and in life, lies and partial stories have a way of coming back with a vengeance. It is possible, however, to limit your personal engagement in these situations. Rita's story is very similar to the corporate scandals of Enron, Tyco, and HealthSouth. These situations were not caused by one person lying. Unfortunately, several people called their own integrity into question when forced to deal with a difficult decision.

It is easy to look at this story and ask what this PM could have done. It was a difficult decision to make. There were several options:

- She could have informed the client of her decision to leave, resulting in a strained relationship with her company.
- She could have come clean with the client immediately after it was revealed, however, this would show that the company intentionally withheld information resulting in a strained relationship with her bosses.
- She could have announced her loyalty to the company, but the client would feel that she was being disloyal to them.

People's strengths can be their greatest weaknesses. Rita's strength was relationship building. Her client not only felt but also believed that she truly cared for them. It is hard not to feel betrayed when a relationship is developed that deeply and the contact seemingly does not trust you enough to reveal this important information. In the end, the point that really seemed to upset the client the most was that Rita continued to accept meeting invitations and make commitments. They felt that she could have declined those events without revealing the information. If too many questions or cancellations began to raise suspicions, she could have referred them to the company. In that situation, she would have forced an earlier reveal, but without breaking her word. When she accepted the invites and commitments knowing that she would not be there, the client felt that she broke her word.

If you are caught in a situation in which you have not revealed all of the information or have not told the truth, there is only one thing you can do. Admit what you did and take the punishment, whatever it may be, and allow it to be a personal scar. Project management, as said earlier, is a collection of scars, and great PMs have many stories to tell. The only thing you can really do in a situation when you are caught in a lie is to own up to it, and call it a lesson learned.

TURNING AROUND FAILING
PROJECTS

N ow that we've addressed how to understand yourself and the people you're working with, as well as how to maintain honesty in the process, let's turn to one of the largest problems in the project management industry. Failure. The statistics are staggering: the propensity for project failure is enormous. The general accepted failure rates range from as low as 59 percent to an unbelievable 94 percent of projects failing to meet their goals. When studying project failure, survey questions are used to try to determine if the project met the desired scope, time frame, or all of the requirements that the project set out to complete. These points all take on new meanings, however, when you consider something Rob Thomsett says in his book entitled *Radical Project Management*:

"Projects fail because of context, not because of content."

If this statement is correct, then a large part, if not the entire 59 percent to 94 percent, of projects failed due to improper setting of expectations.

The teams involved may have delivered on the contents of the project but failed to deliver on the expectations of time and cost, which drastically changes the landscape of the meaning of *project failure*. Now, pair Rob's definition with the Project Management Institute's® belief that a poor project schedule or inadequate budget is the direct result of poor project management, and project failure ultimately rests on the project manager's (PM) shoulders.

It is usually assumed that a project is being run in the first place by a trained PM. Most of the time, however, someone is managing a project along with his or her other duties and things slip through the cracks. In this chapter we consider how to turn around a failing project, no matter the reason.

▨ How to Spot a Project That Is on Its Way Down

The first task in turning around a failing project is to learn how to recognize when a project is failing. In many cases, you need to start with the first step of the classic 12-step program; the first step is admitting that there is, in fact, a problem, such as:

1. **Poor project planning or no plan at all.** It has been said that a failure to plan is a plan for failure. If you do not prepare for problems, they will surely derail you and your project. A project without a clear plan has little chance of success.
2. **Disagreement on project requirements.** Lacking good documentation of requirements or receiving different answers from different team members about the goals of the project muddies the waters. Such issues make it difficult for a project to succeed, because no one is really clear on what success means in this instance.
3. **Lack of team involvement.** Sponsors, stakeholders, or team members are not involved in team activities or are not responding to inquiries about the project. When people are not involved in the project, it has no real life.
4. **Lack of a clearly defined end.** Have you ever had a project last a year, and every time you asked how much longer will the project last, the answer was "just another 2 to 3 weeks"? Failing to set a clear end point means a project will never end, and if it never ends, it can never truly succeed.

5. **Unrealistic demands.** If I said I needed you to rebuild the Eiffel Tower from the ground up for $30 in 3 weeks with five 7-year-old children as laborers, you would laugh. As ridiculous as this may sound, real demands as ridiculous as this have been set for projects. A project with demands that can never be met is sure to fail.

6. **Failure to stop or plan again.** Any time a new PM is assigned to a project, one of the first things that she wants to do is to stop the project and assess where she is in the plan or replan in lieu of having a written plan. A team that responds by saying they are almost finished or they are too busy to plan is a clear sign of a project on the way down. Every team needs to be able to stop and rethink the project's plan.

These are all general theories, and an Internet search will bring up many sites that have early warning signs, causes for failure, or theories as to why projects fail. The funny thing is that PMs seem to make the same mistakes over and over. The whole point of a project management process and profession is to continually improve, but the reasons for project failure still continue to remain the same. Unfortunately, unless the way the projects are being planned or how the expectations are being set changes, the results are unlikely to change.

▨ Someone Isn't Being Heard

One common reason for project failure is that communication has fallen apart and someone is not being heard. Consider the following example.

Amy was the PM assigned to a support project that had no project management structure. The project was consistently not meeting the customer's expectations, and senior management wanted a plan to improve customer satisfaction. Amy started to investigate the root causes of the satisfaction issues. She met with the team as a whole and then individually. As she met with the team members, the issues were becoming quite clear. The team had already identified the causes of the customer satisfaction issues, and they attempted to put action plans in place to rectify the problems. Amy investigated the options that the team had put together and saw that they were quite viable.

She compiled the information into a presentation and scheduled a meeting with her senior management. She outlined the options and asked for a decision from senior management as to which option they agreed with. They chose an option, and she implemented the plan. There was an immediate improvement in the timeliness of customer service, which in turn led to an improvement in customer satisfaction. As the improvements continued for the next couple of weeks, senior management brought the PM in to thank her for a job well done. They asked how she came up with the options she presented. "I didn't," she replied. "The team developed the options. All I did was examine them for viability and present them to you." The senior management team was in disbelief. They wondered why the team hadn't presented the options to them before this. Amy replied, "They may have not understood the best way to present the information to you or how to approach you with their ideas. But it was their ideas all along."

There are many reasons why the team may not have been able to communicate their options to the management in this example. Teams can develop behaviors based on small insignificant events. At one point, a senior manager could have said "no" too abruptly and demoralized a team member. That team member then begins to have the attitude that senior management doesn't care or will not listen to them. A few episodes of that and groupthink can set in.

According to www.dictionary.com, *groupthink* is defined as:

> "The act or practice of reasoning or decision making by a group, especially when characterized by uncritical acceptance or conformity to prevailing points of view."

or

> "Decision making by a group (especially in a manner that discourages creativity or individual responsibility)."

For a very serious example, groupthink was the cause of the Challenger Space Shuttle disaster. This is no small statement. Groupthink was the ultimate cause of one of the worst space tragedies in our time. When the analysis of the disaster was complete, it was determined that the O-rings in the rocket booster were the cause of the explosion. An engineer at the company warned senior management that when the weather drops below a certain temperature, the integrity of the O-rings is compromised. The engineer asked for more time from senior management to be certain. The panel that was formed to uncover the reasons for the Challenger disaster found some startling information. Originally, the company that made the O-rings recommended that the Challenger should cancel the launch until the temperature rose above 53°F, which was not expected to occur for several days. NASA had already canceled the launch a few times and was under enormous political and societal pressure. NASA applied pressure to the engineering company. Fearing the loss of future revenue and backlash from causing another delay, the engineering company began to question its own data and began to rationalize their decision. The engineering company asked for 5 minutes to discuss the situation. During the 5 minutes that the company was isolated, enormous pressure was put on the engineer about his data and analysis. The question for the company became whether to choose safety and possible loss of revenue or risk future revenue. Inevitably, the pressure to conform outweighed the right decision. When the engineering company called NASA back, they recommended that the Challenger should launch. The official findings of the panel stated that the technical malfunction was the O-rings, but the cause of the disaster was groupthink.

When anyone in management stops listening to their team members, disaster can strike at any time. When a project is failing, first look to the communication. More than 90 percent of a PM's job is to communicate, whether this means documentation, meetings, one-on-one conversation, or phone calls. When you refer to the list of key indicators, communication is a central part of all of the items. When team members are not being heard, project failure is sure to follow. When communications stop, people stop being heard

If people aren't listening, watch for the following signs:

- Make sure that the communication plan established in the beginning of the project is being followed.
- If normally active team members are starting to not show up or are not giving regular updates, make sure that you seek them out to inquire as to why.
- If team members seem distant or are not engaged in team discussions, make sure that you discuss this with them. There are times

when team members will speak up, someone will shoot down their idea or comment, and then they react by refusing to speak up again. Watch for this behavior.

- Do not take no response as acceptance. Passive acceptance can kill a project. Some PMs feel that they can send an e-mail and state, "If I have not heard from you in 3 days, I will assume that you approve and accept this requirement." Active acceptance is required for projects.

Project team dynamics is a science. Like a young seedling, it requires care, growth potential, space to grow, and has to be fed. Project team communications can be the same way. You must watch the communication streams, actively solicit feedback, and grow the team to active participation and communication.

▣ Watch the Ego

There is a great debate in project management as to whether a PM should be an expert in the industry or field in which she is running projects. This is dangerous, as it can become a way of not listening to the team. For example a newly promoted PM named Justin is given a project. Justin used to be a developer, and now he is a PM of an application development project. He assembles the team and asks for estimates of how long items will take to accomplish. One developer estimates 120 hours for a given task. Justin responds, "120 hours? That should be done in only 60 hours! I can do it in 60 hours." The problem with Justin being an expert is that he begins to rely on his own experience versus the team's capabilities. There are many established PMs that will use this same example to support why they should be an expert in the field. They will say that the PM can tell if the developer is padding an estimate. This true, but it is not a complete answer as to whether an expert is more effective. What is clear is that if the PM is the expert, he must keep his ego in check and rely on what the team can do, versus what the PM thinks.

Another area where ego becomes an issue is with the power that comes with project management. One of the greatest advantages of being a PM is easier access and visibility to the executives at the company. One of the worst advantages of being a PM is easier access to the executives. Sometimes with that visibility, a PM can forget that he is an enabler, not the doer—meaning, a great PM works behind the scenes and pushes the team to the front. The PM's job is to ensure that the team members are getting everything that they need to be successful. This topic will be explored later in Chapter 9, but for now, keep in mind that the project team is completing the work.

For instance, Shawn was the new PM assigned to a failing project. His job was to assess what the issues were and implement a plan to get the project back on track. He met with the former PM. When Shawn asked the former PM what he felt the issues were, his reply was, "All this project needs is about five more of me and it will run fine." Shawn quickly discovered what the issue was. The previous PM was so concerned about getting the credit for the project's progress that he stopped communicating with the team. When Shawn took over, he asked team members their opinion about the project, and they responded that the previous PM did not disseminate information, took credit for the positive aspects, and blamed them for those that were negative. He was an ego hound and was only interested in furthering his career. The result was that he stopped listening to the team, lost their confidence, and eventually lost his job.

Recognition and reward are compelling and sought-after results of projects, but watch your ego and ensure that the team is being recognized properly. If not, then you could be the one without a job at the project's completion.

▒ When It's Wrong, It's Wrong

There are times when a PM is assigned to turn around a failing project that simply can't be saved. There are some PMs who feel that project cancellation is a negative issue. Although stopping a project before completion or canceling a project that is bound for failure can seem negative, they are great positives for many companies. Why continue to labor on a project that has dragged on and on with no end in sight and a myriad of problems? Why start an enterprise that will fail? Project Management Institute still teaches a project selection method called a "murder board." Its goal is to try to kill a project before it even begins or to look into all of the issues with the current planning of a project.

Here is an example of when stopping a project is actually the best option. A development project was 6 months behind schedule,

$300,000 over budget, and the client was growing increasingly concerned over its investment. Antonio was the PM assigned to assess progress and create a new plan that would reset the client's expectations. Antonio first asked to see all of the documentation for the project. For software development, some of the key documents are the scope of work, functional specification, and use cases. The team pointed to a collection of more than 100 binders of information along the wall. Antonio first noticed that a team of developers were writing code, but none of them had one of the 100 binders open to refer to the specifications. The project, from a scope standpoint, was a relatively simple application. Although it was not unheard of, Antonio was concerned about why an application that seemed simple would need 100 binders of documentation. Also, if it was complex enough to warrant that level of backup, why were the developers not using it?

The answers became quite clear. The salesperson sold the technology improperly. Instead of gracefully backing away from the project, the team tried to make a square peg fit into a round hole. When it didn't fit, they wrote reams of documentation to shave, chip away at, or otherwise force the square peg through. Upon realizing this, Antonio called his senior management and asked to stop the project. It didn't matter if they could eventually get the square peg in the hole; the project should have never been sold in the first place. Antonio wanted it stopped.

After some convincing, senior management eventually agreed and a long battle ensued. In the end, Antonio's company lost a tremendous amount of money and face. If they had continued down the path they were on, however, the customer would have bought a highly customized, overworked, and diamond-encrusted square peg that fits one type of round hole. Should the customer ever change his or her mind, the project would have had to have been redone. The closing of the project was painful, but it should never have been begun in the first place. Greed took over, and the salesperson saw dollar signs that he could not pass up; however, when it's wrong, it's wrong.

■ Stopping a Project Before It Starts

Another way to turn around a failing project is to stop it before it even begins. This is another case when sometimes someone in sales or a sponsor creates a project that is doomed from the beginning. For example, a PM named Michael was assigned to implement a new software program for a client. The client demanded that a project plan be completed prior to the first meeting with the PM. Without input from the team, Michael created a plan that mirrored the newly signed scope of work. Michael sent the plan to the client. When Michael arrived, the client already seemed agitated. The following conversation ensued:

CLIENT (C): "Your project plan has the project finishing in October. Your salesperson said that it could be completed by June."

MICHAEL (PM): "We can certainly look at our options. I used the signed scope of work as the guideline for duration and stages within the plan. Based on the information provided in the signed document, the project would end in October."

C: "Your salesperson said that it would be done in June and that the scope of work was just something we needed to execute to get started. We didn't have time to change the paperwork to reflect what needed to happen."

PM: "Okay. Let's see how we can get this done. Our normal time frame to complete the technical design and architecture is 4 weeks. Then, the installation of the software will use the design as its guide and that takes 2 weeks. Those two tasks will take us past June and they need to occur in that order."

C: "The salesperson said that we can install and configure the software while the design and architecture was occurring."

PM: "You would like us to install and configure the software without a design?"

C: "No. We want a design, but we want to do it at the same time."

PM: "The design is required to install and configure, so it is normally done before the installation."

C: "Look, we don't care what you do. Just do it by June."

Obviously, Michael was distraught about the conversation. The client was demanding installation prior to the completion of the design which, in Michael's opinion, was a disaster waiting to happen. Michael had experience with the software package and had personal knowledge of failures due to lack of design. He wanted to set up a meeting with the salesperson to discuss the demands. The day of the meeting, the salesperson quit the organization. This left the PM with an unreasonable customer with unreasonable demands and a plan for failure. There was only one thing that Michael could think of that would protect his organization and himself. He contacted his manager and told him what had transpired with the client. Michael and his manager set up a meeting with the client to try to reset proper expectations. The client still declined to listen and demanded a June date. The last step was to stop the project.

It took a tremendous amount of courage; however, Michael and his manager were confident that the project would fail. Therefore, they gave the client two options. The first option would be to nullify the deal. The second option was to allow the client access to the technical resources but have the client be responsible for the project management of the installation. In the end, the client took the second option. They still tried to push for the June date and proceeded to direct the installation without design. The result was a failed project. The software did not work as intended and did not provide the value the client was looking for. The review of the project by the client's management determined that the project failed due to lack of proper design. Unfortunately, this is not an isolated incident. The client had blinders on and was overly optimistic that they could complete the project in an accelerated fashion. Instead of recognizing failure early and asking their management for a reprieve on the date or to reconsider the project, they pressed forward. Their fear of failing caused failure.

Many organizations are looking to improve their productivity and resource utilization. They focus on portfolio management, the process that helps ensure that the organization is working on the right projects. The advent of portfolio management implies that many projects that are currently underway may not be adding true value to the organization. This story is an example of that. The time and resources that were wasted working on a project that was doomed to fail was a result of failing to stop a bad project before it started. Many organizations feel that they do not have time to plan. The lack of planning leads to poor execution and wasted resources. The reality of the loss is greater than just the failed project. There is also the loss of what could have been done if the resources were properly aligned. Portfolio management is a newer concept that continues to grow out of the lack of project execution management. More and more executives are becoming more directly involved in monitoring project progress. Their hope is to execute great projects and stop the bad ones or those that lack value before they begin.

▓ "It Is What It Is"

This book does not imply that if the PM says it, senior management will do it. This is not always the case. Sometimes, you have to adopt the attitude of "It is what it is" and report appropriately. You must understand that even with the best plans, options, arguments, and facts, senior management still may not do what is being requested. They may continue down a wrong path. In these cases, proper project management can still be followed, and the truth will eventually come out.

A project was failing, and Dion, the new PM, was the fourth person assigned. Dion had a reputation of being able to turn around the impossible, and senior management was tired of the lack of progress on the project. Dion assessed the situation and developed a plan. The team had told him that the project's progress was extremely slow due to the working conditions. They were developing software with their client who was in one state, the server that they were working on was in another, and they were located in a third state. There were three developers, all trying to get to one server. If one developer made a mistake, it would corrupt the development environment, and the server would also lose the work that the other developers were completing. This was happening often. The team stated they felt that they would get at least a 75 percent productivity boost if the server could be located where they were or at least if an interim server could be located with the development staff that would communicate with the server in the other state. It made perfect sense to Dion. He presented the options to the senior manager who was acting as the internal sponsor on the project. The senior manager immediately shot down the idea. No explanation was given. The senior manager then demanded that Dion come up with a new plan and a new schedule for completion and get back to him immediately.

Dion went back to the team somewhat dejected but continued to do the work. He sat with the project team and received new estimates on how long the project would take to complete, but he had to account for the corruption issues that were occurring in the development environment. This problem extended the project much further than the senior manager had originally anticipated. When presented with this information, the senior manager said, "No way! We are going to change our whole development methodology! We have a client call in 30 minutes, I will handle this!" The senior manager then took over the customer call.

He told the customer that the team had decided that the customer's input and changes were delaying the project and that they would be changing the development methodology. The new methodology will not allow the client to see the project until it was completely finished, and it would be complete in 3 months.

The team estimated 6 months, and changing the methodology would extend that estimate even further. The project team was just committed by the senior manager to do twice the work planned in half the time estimated to do the original work.

Dion re-estimated the project and showed that the new mandates were not possible under the current environment with the present development staff. They either needed more resources or to have the server located with the team. Again, the senior manager rebuffed Dion and declared that he was the fourth PM on this project, and he could get a fifth if Dion didn't comply with his demands. Dion knew that he was fighting a losing battle but continued to do everything possible to try to bring the situation in line. A conference call was scheduled with the senior manager and his boss. Dion tried on several occasions to work out the differences with the senior manager before the conference call. He left voice mails for him. The call would be returned to the team leader, who would be sitting right next to Dion. The senior manager would ask the team leader what Dion wanted. When the team leader said he was unsure but that Dion was right next to him, the senior manager said he would call Dion right back. He never called.

The conference call with the senior manager and his boss was an unbelievable event. When they all were on the phone, Dion outlined the issues that he saw with the project. The senior manager acted surprised. He said things like, "I'm really disappointed with you. I had assumed you would bring issues like these to my attention." He then went on to lecture Dion about proper project management techniques and how the communication needed to be better. Dion was stunned, as he had been bringing these things to the senior manager's attention and was either berated, ignored, or belittled every time. The conference call ended. Dion felt alone, confused, and at risk of losing his job. He then employed the "it is what it is" attitude. He came to a decision that if he was at risk of his losing job, he would lose his job on his terms. He called the senior manager's boss and shared with him all of the documented occurrences. The key point was that the project had four PMs and all were failing. What hasn't changed was the internal leadership or the development staff.

At the end of the call, the senior manager was taken off of the project. Dion then began to report to the senior manager's boss for project progress. There was still tremendous damage to the customer relationship, the team morale, and Dion's confidence throughout the ordeal, but at least the major roadblock to project success had been removed.

This story proves that even if the right theories and fundamentals are followed, a lack of (or poor quality of) the executive leadership can still cause a project to fail. Although Dion was putting together plans and trying to turn the project around, the senior manager was taking the project off course. The moral of the story is to stick to the fundamentals. When faced with a situation in which you can't change the way the project is being handled:

- Focus on identifying the problem.
- Assess the impact.
- Create options.
- Get agreement for those options to deal with project issues (even if the option means you have to replace a senior manager).

A central theme to project management is a cycle of project phases. There are five distinct phases in project management:

- Initiation
- Planning
- Executing
- Controlling
- Closing

Initiation and closing stand alone. Planning, executing, and controlling is a cyclical process that continues throughout the life of the project. The four points listed previously are the steps that complete the cycle.

The "it is what it is" strategy is a core theme throughout this book. It is utilized in dealing with mandated dates, creating proper risk assessments, writing project plans, and dealing with difficult situations. We'll also discuss with regard to putting plans into action and communicating great information. It will all revolve around the reality of the situation and how to bring a halt to common project issues. If so many projects fail, then the reason must be that they were not planned properly in the first place. The theories found in the next several chapters will validate the "it is what it is" strategy and will help repair the broken processes in project management practice.

How to Assess the Current Situation and Create an Action Plan That Works

One of the key reasons that projects can fail is due to the decline of communication, which also leads to the team members not being heard. Therefore, the best way to assess the current situation is to establish and meet the team's needs. For instance, Candy was the PM assigned to turn around a failing software development project that had only two developers. When she arrived on site and introduced herself, the first developer was quite rude and announced, "I will not work an ounce of overtime for you. Just so you know." The second developer said, "I'll work all of the overtime you want, as long as you pay me." Taken aback, Candy continued with her introductions. She felt a bit awkward, but she did not judge the team right away. The project had been failing. The team was demoralized, and she was a new authority figure.

Her first order of business was to assess the situation. The project was behind schedule. Candy found it peculiar that the project was behind and a developer was declaring that he would not work overtime. All projects are different, but a standard process to turn around a project is:

1. Stop the current progress and begin a replanning effort.
2. Determine the progress made to date and estimate the work and durations remaining.
3. Determine impact to the other project management plans (cost, schedule, risk, communications, etc.)
4. Re-publish the plan and reset expectations.

There are many variations to those steps, but in essence, that is what is required to begin to turn around a project. If step three is surprising, understand from a project management standpoint, a plan consists of much more than just a schedule. To read more about the various plans, refer to *Project Management Body of Knowledge*® that is issued by Project Management Institute.

Although Candy followed the first two steps and understood the level of effort required to complete the project, she still needed to understand how to most effectively divide the tasks. She had to understand why the first developer was against overtime, so she asked him. He stated that he had been working so many hours and had performed so much overtime, yet the project was still behind schedule. His experience was that no matter how much overtime he put in, he still would never finish in the time frame allotted. Candy understood that he was not motivated by money but by quality of life. Therefore, she put together a plan. She talked through the estimates that she had just received from him. She questioned and ensured that the estimates in terms of hours to complete the work were accurate. She then put together this thought:

"I'll make a deal with you. I promise that I will not schedule more tasks than will fill an 8-hour day for you based on the estimates that you have given me. If you finish early, you can go home early. I will pay you for 8 hours, but if the work takes you more than 8 hours, then I need you to stay here until you are finished. Fair?"

The developer quickly agreed. To be fair, she offered the same deal to the other developer. The second developer declined. He wanted as much overtime as possible. Now she had a better understanding of the people she would be working with. She then looked at her plan and developed her critical path. The critical path for a project consists of tasks, which if delayed, would cause the project to end late. In a project, not all tasks are on the critical path. For example, if you are building a house, pouring the foundation, building the frame, and finishing the house are all on the critical path. Installing the mailbox, although important, isn't really dependent on the house itself being completed, therefore, it is not on the critical path. If a PM wants to complete a project early, he or she looks first to shortening the duration of a task on the critical path.

Understanding this methodology, Candy chose to place developer two, the one that would work overtime, on all critical path tasks. Developer one was scheduled to as many noncritical path tasks as possible. The end result was a project that finished 3 weeks before the end date and a project that was successfully turned around.

The lesson of this chapter is that although project failure is a huge problem in the industry, it is not something you should just throw your hands up about and give up on. There are definite strategies and approaches you can use to turn around a project that is heading for failure.

DEFINING THE WORD *DONE*

The word *done* is a confusing point in project management situations. There are 10 definitions for it at www.dictionary.com. Some of the varied dictionary meanings include "worn out," "cooked completely," "finished," "exhausted," and "dead." The word *done* is such a simple word, but it can lead to a tremendous amount of miscommunication about project completion. Getting a grip on how projects are completed and what terminology is used can help you become a more efficient project manager (PM), with more successful projects.

■ Definition of *Done* in Project Management

One of the first things a PM should do is to define the word *done*. When team members announce that they are "done," what does that mean? If it is a software development project, have they tested the code? Have they deployed it? Can you see it? Or does it mean that they are done with the coding only and have to move on to the next step?

Take for example, PM Ted who was working with his support team for a large software development project. The sales manager asked if the coding of the application was done. Ted answered, "We are done with the development." A few days later, the sales manager brought the customer in unannounced and asked Ted to show the customer the finished product. Ted was dumbfounded. He said, "The product isn't ready to be shown just yet." The customer was immediately upset. He looked at the sales manager and said, "I thought you said it was done!" The sales manager pointed to Ted and said, "He said it was done!" Ted quickly replied, "I said we were done with the development. We still have four more stages to go before the customer can see it. After development, we go to unit test. Once we pass unit test, there is integration testing, quality assurance, documentation, and then we test it for the user. We still have 4 weeks to complete these activities, and we are planning on being done right on time." The customer said, "On time? Based on the sales manager telling us we could see it, we assumed we were at user testing and could move our launch date up. Our marketing department moved the launch up a whole month!"

This is a true story that cost the development company over $350,000 in damages. How many assumptions were made?

- The sales manager assumed the entire product was done and told the customer.
- Ted assumed that the sales manager understood what "The development is done" meant.
- The customer thought that the product was done and it was time to start testing.
- The customer also assumed that if the product could be tested, it would be done sooner.

All of these points stem from the original misunderstanding. Many project problems can be tracked back to the definition of the word *done* as the initial point of misunderstanding.

Many different types of projects can suffer from this misunderstanding. A rule of thumb: The more complex the team is, the more effort will be required for the communication and coordination. If the team consists of workers from multiple disciplines, then you may have people who use different definitions for the same term. Think of building a home. There are carpenters, electricians, plumbers, general contractors, inspectors, roofers, concrete pourers, and many more workers. They all have requirements that must be completed before they can start their own specific task, and they also have others waiting for them to finish before different jobs can start. For example, the electrician needs to have the foundation and frame of the house completed before he can begin his work. Meanwhile, the drywall hanger needs to wait for the electrician to complete the wiring before he can complete his job. If you build a real project plan, which is discussed in Chapter 9, then all of the tasks depend on each other. The word *done* should be the trigger to start the next task.

Team Building with the Word *Done*

The definition of the word *done* can be a great team-building experience. Many team members in the corporate world today feel somewhat dejected, reserved, or nonparticipatory in project planning. The cause for these sentiments is often due to the fact that they feel like their input is not heard, or that they will be told what to do and when to do it instead of being asked what can be done and how long it will take.

David Maister, one of the leading authorities in management theory and tactics, published a study in which employees were asked to rank 10 items based on the importance of each to their job satisfaction. He then asked the employee's managers to rank the same 10 items based on how the managers *thought* the employees would answer. Table 5-1 shows the results of the survey.

The most amazing thing about the survey is that the top three items the employees felt most important are what the managers felt were least important. It shows that the greater the consensus that can be built through team interaction, the better.

For a PM, the first true team consensus can be built by holding a team meeting to define the word *done*. Janet is a PM who passes out index cards and asks the team members to write the definition of the word *done* on the front side. She then tells them to set the cards aside until later. Then, throughout the remainder of the meeting, the team goes on to discuss the project, requirements, and how the planning will

TABLE 5-1. *TOP 10 ITEMS RELATED TO JOB SATISFACTION*

Item	Subordinate Rating	Supervisor Rating
Appreciation for good work	1	8
Feeling "in" on things	2	10
Help with problems	3	9
Job security	4	2
Salary or wages	5	1
Interesting work	6	5
Promotion chances	7	3
Loyalty to/from	8	6
Coworkers	8	6
Working conditions	9	4
Tactful discipline	10	7

occur. The entire meeting is generated to explain to each other what the word *done* will mean to the team. Once they have had this discussion, Janet writes the key definition points into a statement of what *done* will mean on a whiteboard as the team makes decisions. At the end of the meeting, she asks that the word *done* be defined on the back of the index card. She points out that this is the meaning she will hold them all to throughout the course of the project. Then she asks the team members to reflect on the differences between the first and second definition. Janet can point out how the team just came together and built an agreed consensus on the true meaning as it pertains to the project. As simple as it sounds, Janet just made her first huge step toward developing the resources assigned to the project into a project team.

■ How *Done* Can Set Proper Expectations

Once the team has defined the word *done*, the project can really begin its planning process. There are many reasons that expectations are set improperly on projects and many come from misinterpretations of the questions that are being asked. For example, a PM asks a team member the question, "How long will that take to be done?" The answers from the resource can mean a multitude of things:

- The team member could be a veteran and might add time to the estimate based on experience. Veterans tend to have been burned before or have been yelled at before for missing estimates. They also have more experience in dealing with problems and could call on that past experience. Therefore, they tend to inflate the estimate.

- The team member could be a new addition to the team and bring a variable "Name That Tune" (random) approach and try to impress his new manager. His estimate could be quite aggressive and a best-case scenario because he has limited experience on what will work and what will not.

- The team member may account for unknowns or may not.

Because the team has already defined the word *done*, at least they are estimating the same result of the work. Chapter 7 will help refine the estimates of the team. Defining the word *done* refines the particular outcome of the work being provided.

Fortunately, the word *done* is defined, and the team is at least speaking the same language. This begins the process of setting proper expectations. Whether it is the sales manager, PM, customer, or team member, they all have the same understanding.

Lack of Historical Information

Project Management Institute® (PMI) teaches that the first thing PMs should do is look at historical information as a reference to plan projects. Unfortunately, they rarely have a repository of good information to rely on. They may have a project management office or a central location for files that have the proposed project plans and meeting minutes. There is rarely a repository of what was planned versus what really happened, however. If there is a central location for the information, without a definition of what each task was designed to do and what the definition of the word *done* was, it is difficult to ascertain any meaning.

If we can't look to the past and analyze what occurred, how do we continuously improve? A term that many PMs hear is "lessons learned." It is a staple in project management theory, training, and planning. It is supposed to be the last step in any project. The importance of lessons learned is to bring the team together, discuss what went right and wrong, and devise a plan ensuring that the same mistakes are not repeated. Many PMs, however, either do not find the time to complete lessons learned or they do so, but do not have a central repository to keep them for reference. In either case, the information becomes useless. Generally, because nobody feels the impact of completing these lessons, they start skipping this important step.

A great way to determine when a project is "done" could be to hold a meeting that documents what went right and wrong with the project (also known as "lessons learned"). The documentation of this material is then completed and placed in an accessible location for all future PMs.

Creating Lessons Learned

For a project to be done, "lessons learned" must be completed. This is a document created when the team reviews the issues and risks that occurred on a project and documents any lessons they learned so that the next team can avoid making the same mistake or avoid the issue. The problem is that PMs rarely can get their resources to attend a lessons learned meeting (due to time constraints or a lack of belief that the meeting is worthwhile), or if team members do attend, the PM has difficulty pulling the lessons learned out of them. The expectation for completing lessons learned should be set in the beginning. In the first team meeting, the PM is defining the word *done* with the team. This is the perfect opportunity for the PM to state, "My definition of *done* is when the lessons learned document, which gets created in the final team meeting attended by each and every one of you, is created and agreed upon by all." This statement simply sets the expectation with the team that not only will the final document be completed, but that each member will be required to attend and participate.

If the team participates, how do you ensure that you can facilitate a great lessons learned session? To identify topics to discuss, look at any project documentation. Some common forms of documentation are:

- **Project Charter:** This is the document that formally recognizes the project and assigns the PM. Many companies may call this an Initiation Document or a Project Request Form. It is the document that starts the project.

- **Issue and Risk Log:** A PM will normally keep a log of any issues and risks identified on a project. This document is a great source of history, as it will show what other project teams encountered and how they overcame the problems.
- **Status Reports:** A PM will create a regular report outlining the status of a project. Researching these documents can help pinpoint where issues arose and how the overall project progressed.
- **Defect Reports:** In software development, a *defect* is something that did not work as expected. Defect reports help track and show resolution of the defects encountered in the project.

These documents will help your team identify problems that occurred and could have been avoided. Ask each team member to contribute at least one example of lessons learned to the meeting.

Set the expectation of a lessons learned meeting when the project first begins. Make sure everyone understands it is neither a blame session nor designed to air out the personal differences of the team. It is implemented to improve the overall project process. Make sure that everyone on the project gets a copy of the completed document, so they can see the results of the meeting.

The greatest way to ensure that lessons learned become ingrained in the project process is to reference them in the first team meeting of the next project. There will be a point, if this step is diligently followed, when a potential project disaster will be averted due to experience from a previous project. When that occurs, make sure that it is widely known and offer great praise to the team that documented the item from the previous project. As soon as the team sees that this process will inevitably save future project pain, they will gladly participate in the next session.

APPLICATION OF THE IRON TRIANGLE (TRIPLE CONSTRAINT)

The *iron triangle* is a metaphor for the interdependence of the different variables that work together and compete with each other to create a project. The iron triangle once stood for three core items: cost, schedule, and quality; however, it has now evolved into a number of different configurations. These configurations were designed to set and measure the expectations of a project. Originally, it was used as a measure of project success. Time has shown that the iron triangle is an inadequate way to measure success. To be truly functional, it should be used for setting project expectations but not as a definitive measure of success. The triangle is an important approach to project management because it helps showcase the effect that the different parts of a project have on each other.

▇ What Is the Iron Triangle?

Although there are many configurations of the iron triangle, the most commonly used definition is cost, schedule, and quality. Some people have replaced the words *cost* with *resources* and *schedule* with *time*. When thinking of the iron triangle, visualize the three sides. Assign a term to each side. The triangle shows the balance between the three core parts of a project. The three items intersect, and as the focus on one side shortens or lengthens, the other two sides of the triangle have to shorten or lengthen to accommodate. When it comes to setting the expectations for the project, this idea works quite well. When you begin to measure project success, however, the triangle begins to fail. It fails because there are many more factors to consider.

The triangle was named the *iron triangle* because although the sides can shorten or lengthen, they are unbreakable. They can ebb and flow as needed, but the three sides are in constant contact and must adjust as the other sides do.

Many theorists are now questioning whether the three items are enough. New definitions are forming for the iron triangle. There are many arguments as to what constitutes the three sides because a fourth element, scope of work, is also prevalent. Some books will teach the iron triangle as cost, scope, and time with quality as the central focus. Others will teach it as this book does, as cost, schedule, and quality with the additional focus on the scope of work; however, one other element is missing: customer service. So now there are five things that can measure a project success. There are new theories being discussed that show 10 items within the "triple constraint" of the iron triangle.

Why the Triangle Works

The triangle is representative of the way a real project works. The three sides of a triangle are mutually dependent on each other, just as the three factors of a project are mutually dependent on each other as well. A change on one side of the triangle will affect at least one of the other sides. Let's take a look at the effects focusing on each side can have:

> **Cost Focus:** If cost is the focus, then quality or resources will need to be adjusted. Usually when there is a focus on cost, it is due to budget constraints. If a project has an unlimited budget, then cost is rarely a factor; however, if cost is constrained, then key decisions must be made. To limit cost, the project

may have to use more inexpensive resources, reduce quality cycles, or cut testing in order to meet the budget.

Schedule Focus: If time is of the essence, then quality or cost will need to be adjusted. If the schedule needs to be accelerated, then the project manager (PM) could assign more resources to the project causing cost (increasing the amount paid to do the same work) or quality (tougher communication streams) to be adjusted. Sometimes both will be changed. If the project must meet a specific deadline, quality could be cut to meet the accelerated time frame.

Quality Focus: If quality is the most important element, then cost or schedule will need to be adjusted to permit an increase of time or budget. Quality usually affects both other sides of the triangle. A task usually will take longer to complete and thereby cost more because an extra step or process will be required to increase the quality. Think of a five-star restaurant versus a quick short-order diner. Usually, the meal takes longer to cook and costs more at the five-star restaurant.

Depending on the project, the side most constrained will be selected. For instance, if the project is a regulatory or market-driven project, schedule is usually the most constrained. The project must finish at a certain time. For quality projects, cost or time must be allotted to effectively complete them. The interaction most disagreed about in the definition of the iron triangle is that quality increases costs and takes longer to do. Most quality projects are aimed at reducing costs and time to complete.

PM Tan had a project that was to assist in defining service-level agreements and creating standard operating procedures for an organization. One of the first tasks was to present the project deliverables to a team of stakeholders. At the presentation, Tan asked which side of the iron triangle should be his focus. In explaining how selecting one side affects the others, one of the executives disagreed and said, "Implementing quality will reduce cost." Tan agreed that a focus on quality *should* decrease cost overall, but to implement it within in a project will cause it to cost more. He then led the executive through a scenario:

TAN (PM): "Let's talk about installing a personal computer at your organization. Are we having quality issues with that currently?"

EXECUTIVE (EXEC): "Yes. We're having problems because the printers are not set up properly, and applications are not installed when the technician leaves. We then have to call the technician back out to complete the job. It decreases productivity for the technician and the employees receiving the computers."

PM: "To fix this issue, I would suggest a checklist with printouts from the application. When a technician finishes installing the computer, I want him to fill out a checklist. It should include the launch of each installed application and a printed test page. Then, I want the technician to staple all test prints to the checklist and leave it at the desk. When the employee arrives, I want her to sign the checklist (alternatively, she can sign it immediately if she is there) and send it back to a central location. If we printed a test page from every application, would that make you feel more confident that the installation was complete and quality was attained?"

EXEC: "Absolutely!"

PM: "Are the technicians doing that today?"

EXEC: "No."

PM: "So they have to come back and fix these items often?"

EXEC: "Yes."

PM: "To implement this level of quality, every transaction now will take longer to complete. Do you agree?"

EXEC: "Yes."

PM: "And because it takes longer to complete, it costs more per transaction. Correct?"

EXEC: "Yes."

PM: "Therefore, we are both correct. By adding quality (the checklist) to the project, each transaction now takes longer and costs more to complete. It should cost less overall, however, because the focus on quality should reduce the return trips to fix the issues of an incomplete install."

This dialogue provides a simple example of how the triangle works. Once understood, it can become a powerful tool in opening up a critical dialogue with stakeholders and sponsors.

■ How to Implement the Triangle

The first thing to remember is that a PM's role is to facilitate the execution of the project. The role does not include deciding what belongs in or out of a project or saying "no" to a project sponsor. It is appropriate to assess the impact of a change or requirement and explain what is needed to implement them. The easiest way to incorporate the triangle is to draw it on a whiteboard and ask the project team to rank the three items in order. Essentially, pick two because one is going to slide. In the example you just read, Tan and his executive had a discussion about the iron triangle. Tan had explained the concept and was trying to implement it.

EXEC: "If anything can be done, then I want a new computer on the desk of an employee within 5 minutes of it breaking."

PM: "It can be done. The question is, will the cost of doing this warrant this level of service?"

EXEC: "How could it be done?"

PM: "We could purchase three computers per employee and have them back each other up every five minutes. We could then put a technician within five minutes of every computer and a technician to back him up. When a computer breaks, the technician will swap it with a new one. If two break in the same area at the same exact time, the second technician will take care of that one. The question is, do you want to pay three times the cost for a computer and pay for 500 technicians to be standing around just in case? There has to be a balance between wants and needs and how they will affect cost, schedule, and quality. In the end, is an hour between a break and a fix acceptable?"

EXEC: "Fair enough."

Tan was hired to work with the organization to help teach and create service level agreements. The project team started with the computer ordering and setup process. At the beginning of the engagement, the business asked for a 2-day turnaround from the point they ordered the computer to the point that it was sitting on the employee's desk for use. Through the application of the iron triangle, asking for tradeoff decisions, and going through the entire process, the business and IT department agreed on 12 business days. The business thought they wanted that level of service, but they were not willing to pay for it.

As discussed in Chapter 4, when a change occurs or a decision needs to be made, a PM must assess the impact and create options. It is not the PM's role to say "no." This does not imply, however, that a PM should blindly agree to stakeholder demands. The PM's role is to show the impact of the demands on the project's three core items: cost, schedule, and quality—and create a balance between them.

■ Use the Triangle for Discovery and Scoping

Once understood, the iron triangle can become one of the most powerful tools a PM has for discovering the motivations of each stakeholder and how well the project is understood. Asking which of the three sides is the most important creates a dialogue between the PM and the stakeholders. It also becomes a powerful tool to see how aligned the stakeholders are with each other.

For example, PM Ahmed was given an assignment that was one of the top three strategic projects for an organization. It had visibility to the top of the company and would be important in setting the direction for the company over the next 5 years. The stakeholders included the chief executive officer (CEO), chief information officer (CIO), and chief financial officer (CFO). Ahmed wanted to uncover the motivations of the leadership team, so he met with each executive individually. The following motivations were uncovered:

CEO: Selected cost as the most important, schedule as second, and quality third. If there were tradeoff decisions, the quality of the application could be worked on after implementation, so it was not as important.

CFO: Selected cost as the most important, quality second, and schedule third. He believed that the schedule could suffer as long as the application was done correctly and the costs were controlled.

CIO: The CIO was the sponsor of the application, and he selected schedule as the top priority, quality as second, and cost as third.

He felt that the longer it took to implement the application, the more the company would lose in productivity and revenue. Therefore, cost was the third concern because he felt all costs would be recuperated in a timely fashion.

This scenario provided great insight for Ahmed. The entire leadership team was divided equally as to what was important. The CEO and CFO were both cost conscious and thought that quality or schedule could be sacrificed, but they disagreed as to which concept ranked second and third. The CIO was willing to sacrifice cost to meet time demands. Before we discuss the outcome of the conversations, what would have happened if Ahmed didn't ask about the priorities?

- If and when a tradeoff decision was required, the stakeholders would likely have had conflicts. For example, if the budget was nearing capacity, the CIO would gladly have run costs over while the CEO and CFO would have wanted to limit functionality or testing.
- Most likely, the CEO and CFO did not understand the benefits of the application because they were willing to reduce schedule or quality to save cost. If they understood the benefits of the project, maybe they would be in line with the CIO.
- Conversely, maybe the CIO believed too highly in the return on costs the application would bring.
- Depending on the situation, whatever decision was made would likely upset two of the three in the leadership team.

The outcome of the conversation was a fantastic discussion. After Ahmed realized that the executives would not make the same decisions given the situation, he brought them together for a key meeting. Once there, he discussed each executive's answers and asked what their rationales were for selecting the order of the components of the iron triangle. Each executive discussed his thought process. All three gained insight and understood the rationale of why each had made their decisions. This talk allowed Ahmed to create a consensus on what would occur or which factor would win given a situation in which a tradeoff decision was necessary. Achieving the consensus an easy because the simple act of asking what was most important facilitated key discussions. The CIO was able to articulate the power of the application, and the CEO and CFO raised their objections. Once the discussion was started, the PM observed, took notes, and facilitated the agreement. Ultimately, the conversation created understanding, which in turn created consensus. Ahmed then knew the direction to take.

In order to truly implement the iron triangle, the PM needs to discuss priorities with the stakeholders. Asking to pick two of the three sides of the triangle in order of importance will show what they feel is most critical to the success. There is no right or wrong answers. Each is based on individual perspective at the time of the conversation. The more disparate answers that are received, the more likely there will be conflict in project crisis situations. To set the proper context for the project, a majority or consensus must be reached as to which factors are most important in managing the project.

■ Why the Triangle Shouldn't Be Used for Project Success

Originally, the iron triangle was used to measure project success. If an assignment met its schedule, with all requirements, and met the projected budget, it was deemed successful. Like many project management concepts, however, this theory is changing. Many organizations are finding out that projects can meet all time, cost, and quality requirements, yet still be a failure overall. The reason is that the measurements are shortsighted. As an example, consider the following situation: An organization has completed a project with all quality requirements delivered, on time, and under budget; however, the project was a failure.

The PM Tess realized the following facts:

The schedule was met only by asking their employees to work ridiculous hours. Nights, weekends, and 12-hour days were requested and completed.

The budget was kept in line because only salaried workers who were not eligible for overtime worked the long hours. Therefore, the company was getting the work of two and three employees per one employee.

Quality initiatives were received by extending the schedule and not paying overtime.

The project finally failed because of how it is evaluated under an evolving theory called *total project costing*. Total project costing theory looks at the entire project, including the maintenance and support after the "go live" date, to measure project success. An example of what the company could find includes:

- More than 50 percent of the project team left due to the long and uncompensated hours required for the project.
- Due to the turnover of the staff, it cost the company three times the amount projected to support the application. The costs were consumed by training and bringing the new resources up to speed.
- All of the other projects suffered so that this one could meet its date.
- The resources remaining in the company were burned out, and there was a lack of motivation to do another project under the same circumstances. The impact of the project on company morale was significantly negative.

Therefore, total project costing ensures that a PM takes all of the costs, including maintenance, and support, into account when establishing success criteria. The iron triangle can still offer factors for setting the success criteria; however, these should not be the only factors that are measured. There are several new theories that abound about what should constitute project success. The best answer is that success should be decided on a project-by-project basis. A great way to discuss the success criteria is by drawing a triangle on the board. Write cost, schedule, and quality on the sides of the triangle and ask the stakeholders, "Pick two, because one is going to slide."

Once the stakeholders select which side will slide, this choice will assist in project estimation. Knowing which constraint will be stagnant and which can slide will allow the PM to make trade off decisions when preparing the project schedule. The next piece to understand is how to get great estimates to construct the project schedule. The next chapter discusses an integral, but often misused or forgotten concept: PERT (Program Evaluation Review Technique).

PERT METHODOLOGY IN PROJECT PLANNING

Thus far, we have discussed understanding your team, defining project completion, the importance of honesty, and the iron triangle. These are all important concepts that will help lead you to successful project management, but there is more to learn. Let's now turn our attention to PERT—an important project management technique that will further assist you in your quest to complete and excel at your projects.

The acronym PERT stands for Program Evaluation Review Technique, which originated in the engineering profession. It was one of the first methodologies that truly understood the uncertainties that a project can present and created a step-by-step process for how to successfully deliver the project despite the unknowns. PERT was used in the late 1950s with the Polaris missile program. It made such a significant impact, in fact, that it is now a standard for today's U.S. Navy projects. Designed as a control process for projects with numerous tasks, unknowns, and risks, the system focuses efforts on critical tasks, estimating the unknown, and assisting in determining project outcomes.

▨ What Is PERT?

PERT is taught in project management classes and textbooks, and many times, it is referred to as a *formula*. In reality, it's an entire process and one that is familiar to PMs; however, they have learned it as the *project management process*, not as PERT. It consists of the following steps:

- Identify activities and milestones—create a work breakdown structure (WBS) and activity definition. (These concepts will be discussed later in the chapter.)
- Determine activity sequence
- Create network diagram
- Estimate time
- Determine critical path

Many modern project management practices were facilitated and updated using the PERT process. Others may have learned the system as the critical path method. The goal of PERT is to identify the critical path of a project. The definition for *critical path* is the longest path through which represents the shortest amount of time in a project. For example, a project team identifies the tasks in Table 7-1.

Based on the information in the table, a network diagram can be created (Figure 7-1).

Now that the activities or tasks have been sequenced, the critical path can be located. To determine the critical path, follow each branch of the network diagram and determine how long each branch will take. The critical path for this network diagram is that Task A-B-C-D-E will take 15 days. The other path, A-D-E takes 12 days.

TABLE 7-1. CRITICAL PATH

Task	Time to Complete	Dependency
A	3 days	None
B	5 days	Task A must finish
C	2 days	Task B must finish
D	4 days	Task A must finish
E	5 days	Tasks C and D must finish

FIGURE 7-1. NETWORK DIAGRAM.

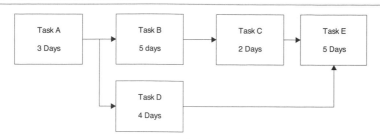

Finding the critical path allows the PM to make many strategic decisions. For example, in the tasks previously listed, if the project needed to be completed 1 day early and the decision was between shortening Task B or Task D, which should the PM choose? The answer is Task B. The reason is because Task B is on the critical path. Shortening Task D will shorten that specific task but will not affect the critical path because the time it takes to complete the project will not change. For example, if the project was building a house and Task B was to frame the house and Task D was to install the mailbox, shortening the time of installing the mailbox will not shorten the overall project because there is nothing else depending on the task to be complete. On the other hand, shortening the time it takes to frame the house will allow the walls to be installed earlier and any other dependent tasks to start earlier. The critical path method identifies the tasks that a PM should focus on to reduce the overall time frame of the project. In addition, the critical path tasks hold the highest risk. If a critical path task is late, the project date will move with it.

The formula of PERT has survived the translations and teachings. although many textbooks leave the process portion out of the text, most books teach the formula for estimation. The formula is (BC + (4*ML) + WC)/6. There are some terminology variances to the formula, but for our purposes, BC stands for best case (also referred to as optimistic), ML stands for most likely, and WC stands for worst case (also referred to as pessimistic.) The premise is that one out of every six tasks will be completed early, one out of every six will finish late, and four out of every six will complete as planned. The formulas also go into greater detail discussing the standard deviations and variances; however, this book will not go into the full realm of the calculations. From a project management strategy, knowing the initial formula will assist you in estimating the cost or effort of the project. The next few sections discuss how to obtain the time estimates and how to use the PERT formula to facilitate setting proper expectations.

■ PERT for Time Estimation

Time estimation on projects is a unique skill. For example, Nathan was a consultant working with an organization to improve their time estimates. He asked one of the participants how long she had worked for the company. She stated 23 years. Nathan asked if she had worked in the same building for 23 years. She replied that she had. He then asked her how long it took her to get to work in the morning. She replied that it took between 30 minutes to an hour. Nathan pondered her answer. He explained that project time estimation is a tough concept. Projects by their nature mean change. Change generally means doing something that has never been done before. Some projects last years. Nathan said, "We are here because this organization wants to establish better practices for time estimation. The reason I was told that I was here is that management is upset that as a team, the company continues to miss their time estimates. However, I think we are placing too much value on time estimates. Why? You have worked in the same building for 23 years. That's 220 working days per year where you've performed the same task, driving to work, more than 5,000 times. Your estimate to this very basic question has 100 percent of variance (30 minutes to an hour) in risk, and yet we expect our staff to commit to us to the hour on how long something will take? There has to be a better way!"

Nathan is right. When PMs ask for time estimates, they are generally asking for a commitment of time and duration for each task. Then they commit the team to a date based on those estimates. Yet the actual tasks are unknown. In essence, the PM is asking the team member to estimate work based on initial understandings.

One thing that can throw off time estimates is the question, "How long will that take?" Basically, the PM asking this question is setting himself up for a game of "Name That Tune!" If he asks a senior level programmer who has been chastised in the past for missing an estimate, the developer may add risk to his answer. If a junior level programmer is asked the question, he may want to establish himself or impress the PM and give a very aggressive estimate. This dilemma is the same as defining the word *done*. The way to get out of the dilemma is to ask at least two more questions. The following conversation illustrates this point:

PM: "How long will it take you to complete this task?"

DEVELOPER: "About 10 days."

PM: "Is that your perfect-world scenario? Will it take 10 days if everything goes as planned?"

DEVELOPER: "No, if everything goes as planned, it should take about 5 days."

PM: "So is 10 days your worst-case scenario? Is that planning for all the things that could go wrong?"

DEVELOPER: "No. I wouldn't see it going past 15 days, but 10 days should be good."

In this conversation, the PM uncovered that the BC = 5 days, ML = 10 days, and WC = 15 days. Applying the PERT formula (5 + (4*10) + 15)/6 = 10 days. The other point of the conversation is that the PM qualified the estimates and understood the entire scenario. It is often the case that the PM will hear additional triggers during this conversation that allows him or her to be more proactive as well. For example, if the PM just asks for an initial estimate without qualification, he or she will usually get one number in return. When the PM qualifies the answer, this forces the developer to think about his or her logic. While thinking of the things that could go wrong, most team members will verbalize issues or roadblocks to completing the task. This is a great source for risk identification for the PM. The PM needs to listen intently during the qualification of time estimates to uncover these areas.

■ How to Factor Risk into the Equation

Risk is a constant struggle for many PMs. Many know that risks are important but they do not always know where to find them, list them, or account for them. Chapter 12 will go in to detail about performing a real risk assessment; however, risk is an important discussion, as it pertains to PERT as well. We have already discussed listening to the team members as their estimates are being qualified, yet there is one more question that can be asked to really identify risk. The question is:

"What makes that your worst case estimate?" Answers could be, "This is a new technology that we have never worked with," or, "The team is geographically dispersed so communication may not be as fast." This type of information will become the basis of when to add risk and when not to.

To further qualify when to add risk or not, let's first understand why this is a consideration. Although risk is accounted for in the PERT formula, there are two types. There is the risk that the team member has simply underestimated the length of the task. There is also the risk that an outside influence could cause the delay. Delineating which risk is which is why the question, "What makes it your worst case?" should be asked.

If the team member states that he is just unsure of how long the task will take, then he or she is adding a buffer. These risks are time risks, and the PERT formula should account for this. Some tasks will finish early, and some will finish late. PERT will assist in accounting for both types.

If the team member states that there is an outside influence, then PERT is generally not handling that risk. For example, if the resource said, "I think 15 days is my worst-case scenario because the part we need is unavailable." This situation constitutes a risk that should be identified and accounted for in addition to PERT. PERT is a fantastic tool to help account for the unknowns in a project and a way to identify critical path tasks. It is also a great way to ask resources to think of everything that can occur and capture risks. In asking your team members to quantify the time estimates, they begin to explain why they have added time to the estimate. The PM now can list the risks that are a result of roadblocks, issues, or outside influences. This list also allows the PM to judge the comfort level of each resource in their estimates. Communication being key, this is a great exercise for a PM to perform with his or her team.

▪ Create a Work Breakdown Structure for PERT

The greater level of detail that is presented, the better chance an accurate estimate can be reached. One of the ways to assist in activity definition is to create a work breakdown structure (WBS). A WBS is a graphical representation of all of the deliverables of a project in which each row represents the entire scope of the project. The goal of the WBS is to

FIGURE 7-2. WORK BREAKDOWN STRUCTURE FOR PAINTING A HOUSE.

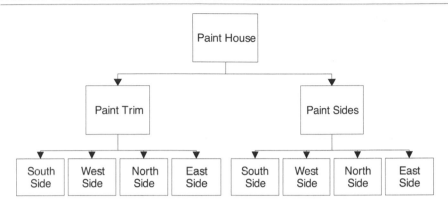

logically subdivide project deliverables into smaller components that are easier to estimate. For example, Figure 7-2 is a WBS for painting a house. This same WBS can be represented as shown in Figure 7-3.

The terms, makeup, or how the items are broken down are not relevant. What is relevant is that the deliverables of the project are broken down into activities that can easily be estimated. In addition to subdividing tasks, there is a rule called the 8/80-hour rule. That is the definition above, or until it makes sense to stop. The key word is *logically*. If a task is estimated to take 160 hours, but it doesn't make sense to con-

FIGURE 7-3. ALTERNATE WORK BREAKDOWN STRUCTURE FOR PAINTING A HOUSE.

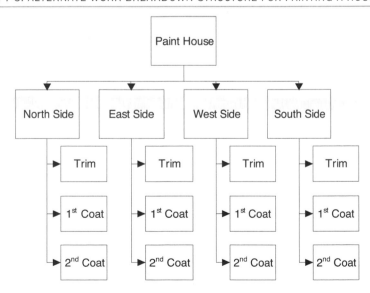

tinue to subdivide the task, then it is acceptable to stop there. Once all tasks have been divided to fit logical sense or the 8/80-hour rule, then the estimates are gathered. This is a type of bottom-up estimation that creates a more educated estimate. The WBS is an activity to be performed by the project team. It is not something a PM should do individually. The benefits of creating a WBS are:

- Team members understand the deliverables of the project.
- Conversation and interaction between team members begins.
- Team members see how their contribution benefits the project as a whole.
- The risk of missing work or allowing tasks to slip through the cracks is mitigated through team discussion.

▨ Examples of PERT in Action

PERT is also a great way to assist a company in selecting a fair fixed-cost price or one cost for the entire project. Many times in business, companies must bid and agree to finish a project for one negotiated price up front. This approach can be quite nerve-wracking for many companies due to the level of uncertainties that follow any project. If projects are known to fail, then agreeing to complete one with one price is a difficult pill for some to swallow. In the case of a fixed-price contract or a contract that sets one price for the whole project up front, the PERT formula should be the central point. It can drive many decisions and establish the amount of risk in a plan.

For example, Ron was a PM contracted to develop a plan and a fixed-cost price for the upgrade of a software package on a client's computer systems. Ron felt that the WBS should be subdivided to the most detailed level so that the risk would be mitigated by subdividing the tasks. In addition, the project consisted of a repetitive series of tasks. To estimate this time frame necessary, the team created a WBS for the activity of installing the software.

The team started by defining what the task "Install the Software" meant. Figure 7-4 represents what they decided.

As the team looked at the WBS, they quickly realized all of the items that they would have potentially missed had Ron asked, "How long will it take to install the software?" They most likely would have

FIGURE 7-4. WORK BREAKDOWN STRUCTURE FOR INSTALLING SOFTWARE.

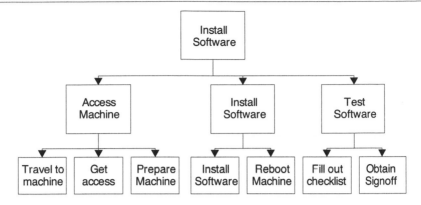

estimated only one of the seven tasks it actually took. The next step was to obtain estimates for all the tasks (Table 7-2).

Utilizing PERT, the team estimated that each machine would take roughly 30.5 minutes to complete this task. The next piece was to look

TABLE 7-2. TIME ESTIMATES FOR TASKS

Task	Best Case	Most Likely	Worst Case	Result	Comment
Go to workstation	1	5	5	4.33	This constitutes the time it takes to physically move to the next machine.
Get access to machine	0	2	15	3.83	The best-case scenario is that nobody is actively working on the machine so the technician can immediately work.
Prepare machine for software installation	0	5	15	5.83	The best-case scenario is that the machine is ready. The worst-case scenario is that it may need to boot up or close active applications.
Install software	3	3	3	3	The software takes 3 minutes to install.

(continued)

TABLE 7-2. TIME ESTIMATES FOR TASKS (CONTINUED)

Task	Best Case	Most Likely	Worst Case	Result	Comment
Reboot machine	2	4	30	6	The worst-case scenario needs to account for slow reboot times or errors.
Fill out checklist	2	4	6	4	
Obtain signoff	0	1	5	1.5	In the worst-case scenario, the technician needs to track down the customer for a signature.
Totals	8	24	79	30.5	

All estimates are in minutes.

at the risk factors that the team discussed during the estimation process. One of the technicians stated that when he was thinking of his worst case, he wanted to know if he should include the observation that about 10 percent of the time, the application would have to be de-installed and re-installed due to various errors. Ron noted the risk and asked the technician not to include that in his estimates. Ron wanted to validate the claim and assess it as an overall risk. After talking with the other technicians, the team could show a trend where 10 percent of the installations had to be redone. Taking this into account, Ron did not want to include the risk in the PERT estimation. Because it was a complete reinstall, he decided to apply the risk to the number of installations. The customer asked for 100 installations. From a risk perspective, Ron factored in 110 installations to account for the risk of issues. The technicians cost $100 per hour. Ron set the fixed-price cost of $5,591 (110 machines multiplied by 30.5 minutes divided by 60 minutes multiplied by $100 per hour).

In the end, the project was completed with 105 installs and took 52 hours. The PM was under budget by a little over 3 hours. One machine took more than 2 hours to install due to various issues. As an average, the time per machine was 31.2 minutes. The PERT methodology allowed Ron's team to account for a variety of outcomes and miss their overall estimate by 42 seconds a machine. It is easy to see why the U.S. Navy utilizes the PERT methodology as a standard in their project management practices.

Now that you understand the process of PERT, the next chapter will move away from formulas and into some soft skills that deal with working with customers to delineate and achieve project goals. All of the skills gathered in this book culminate in the ability to become a great PM.

CUSTOMER FOCUS STARTS WITH GREAT REQUIREMENTS

There is no question that the ability to focus a project will help achieve success. Exactly how you do that is the question much of the time. This chapter directs our attention toward working with the customer.

Often, a project will take on a life of its own. It grows, changes, and becomes its own living organism. During this metamorphosis, the original intent of the project can be lost in translation, and the customer's needs can be obscured. It is important to never lose sight of the customer. Great service comes from setting high standards. Like many project management concepts, requirements are also important when setting expectations—however, whose expectations should be set? This chapter discusses setting great requirements, understanding the difference between technical and functional, and grasping who the true customer is.

▓ Characteristics of Good Requirements

We have already discussed the context and content of a project. In Chapter 4, we examined how most projects fail because of the context of the project, not the content. Setting great requirements ensures that the content of the project is successful as well. Sometimes, these requirements are quite difficult to set. If they are not, the end of the project can never truly be agreed upon. There are several checkpoints a project manager (PM) can put in place to validate whether the requirements are good ones.

Checkpoint No. 1: Make sure that the requirements are clear, concise, and measurable. They must not waiver or be open to interpretation. For example, many projects have a goal of "improve customer satisfaction." This is a fantastic goal for a project, but how exactly will the improvement be made?

- If the assignment is in a call center taking phone calls from customers, will the project be successful if one customer's call is answered 1 second faster?
- Will it be successful if 10 people get the answer they are looking for on the first call?
- What constitutes an improvement in customer satisfaction?
- What is the measurement to ensure success?

If there are 50 team members, then there will be 50 interpretations, and all 50 may be correct. There must be some qualification, definition, and validation to ensure a measurable goal. This same requirement can be written to say, "To improve customer satisfaction, the overall average call answer speed must be reduced by 1 second, and overall first-call resolutions must improve by 10 percent." Setting a measurement allows the team to move on to fulfilling the requirement. The next questions from the project team should then be focused on how to meet the requirement, not on what the requirement means.

Checkpoint No. 2: What is the material worth or value of the requirement? If the statement were removed, would it change the scope of the project?

- If the answer is "yes," then it is a material requirement.
- If the answer is "no," it should not be included in the scope.

Furthermore, unnecessary requirements can create confusion and questions that are irrelevant to the overall scope of the project. These requirements are generally included because stakeholders or the project team feel they need to be overly explicit in the description. The best way to describe this situation is to imagine your requirements for a perfect spouse. Would you list "must be breathing" or "human"? Most likely not. It is not necessary to list everything, just the relevant items.

The other type of requirement lacking material worth is one that is too broad or which is a catchall. For example, a customer wanted a new Web site application. One of the requests was, "all existing functionality of the current Web site." At the end of the project, there were disagreements about project completion. The customer pointed out a database that was not included. The PM for the developing company explained, "That's not part of the project." The customer stated, "It's part of our existing Web site." When the PM looked into it, it turned out the customer had added a new database to their Web site while the developing company was completing their work. The customer was technically right that the database in dispute was on their current Web site, however, it was added after the agreement was signed with the developing company. The requirement that was used for this project was too broad, but the developing company had to adhere to the demand. A better-worded requirement would have been "all functionality of the current Web site as of the date of the agreement."

Checkpoint No. 3: Validate proper interpretation of the requirement. If more than one person reads it, will it mean the same thing? For example, if a requirement was for a system to send a notification to the user when an issue is assigned to them, what does that really mean? The message can be sent by e-mail, faxed, text messaged, or set up in an application inbox. Which method is correct? As stated before, all of the answers are correct. The key is to be specific enough to bring everyone to the same conclusion but not overly specific as to make it an unnecessary or irrelevant requirement. In this example, the message should read, "When an issue is assigned to a person in the system, the system will notify the user by sending an e-mail to the address on record."

Checkpoint No. 4: Ensure the requirements tie directly back to the scope document. For example, the project scope statement is "Book a family vacation for 5 nights in a tropical location for a budget of $7,500." The specifications are clear and concise. Creating a list of vacation spots to travel in the next 5 years may be nice and a fun activity, but it is outside the scope of the current project. Checking the prices of a European vacation could create alternatives, but again, it is not germane to the situation. In many ways, it is like an earmarking bills and budgets submitted in American politics. A U.S. senator may create an earmark of $100,000 to be appropriated somewhere else and include it in a bill or vote that is focused on something else. They try to slide it in so that they do not have to create separate legislation. If the requirement does not tie directly back to the scope, then it should not be a requirement.

The four tests for ensuring that project requirements are sound are:

- Make sure the requirements are clear, concise, and measurable.
- Validate the requirement by removing it from the project to judge its effect on scope.
- Have other people read the requirement to validate that they each come to the same conclusion.
- Make sure that there is a direct link between the requirement and the scope.

If the requirement passes the four tests, then it is important and will help make the content worthwhile to deliver.

Functional Requirements Versus Technical Requirements

When discussing the customer's requirements in an information technology project, it is important to break them down into two types: functional and technical. The difference between the requirements is how they are written. A technical requirement explains how the product or task will accomplish the scope. A functional requirement is what actually needs to be done to complete the project. For instance, a functional requirement could be "notify the user by e-mail when a change occurs." The technical requirement would be "upon update of the object, validate that there is a change. If a change has occurred, then look up the user of the record and send an e-mail to the address on file." In essence, the functional requirement describes *what* should be done, while the technical requirement describes *how* it should be done.

The next difference is the perspective from which the requirement should be defined. If the functional requirement is the "what" of the project, it should be written from the user perspective. If the user is to be presented with choices and then decide which option to take, the instruction would be made based on how the user sees the options and what he or she would do to select the desired option. The technical requirement should be written from the developer's perspective. The information should contain how to set the options to be selected, how to physically display the option, and how to store the information selected. A great example is an old programming test that was given to school-aged children to teach them how computers think. The goal was to tell a robot how to make a peanut butter and jelly sandwich. The functional requirement was to make the sandwich. The technical requirement involved the actual making of the sandwich. The teacher would take the instructions and literally follow them step by step. During the demonstration, there would always be some forgotten instruction like "Unscrew the cap from the peanut butter." Because this instruction was forgotten, the teacher would be trying to put the knife into the peanut butter jar and would get stuck because the top was still securely fastened. Technical requirements should also take into account the technical aspects of the project. Key areas that seem to always become issues are performance, availability, and security. These are often missed steps that can kill a project after completion. For example, a company wants Gene, a developer, to create a dashboard that will display key metrics for them so that they can help make critical business decisions faster. Gene delivers the end product, and it shows each metric in exactly the way the company had requested. When a user from the company clicks on one of the metrics, it takes 60 seconds to load the next page. The user says, "This is unacceptable!" Likewise, the company is upset. Yet, how fast the page loads was never a requirement. The only requirement was to display the information, and there was no requirement made about performance or speed. This is a common situation. The performance of an application or solution is just as critical as what the application or solution does, however, it is rarely accounted for.

This also occurs when it comes to the security of an application. There are so many ways to ensure that unauthorized users do not access sensitive data or gain unauthorized use of a system, but protecting against all possibilities is just like purchasing insurance. There are several types that most people have: life, home/renter's, and auto. There are also many other options: annuities, disability, flood, earthquake, fire, accidental death, and dismemberment insurance. The question becomes risk versus reward. Just as often happens with purchasing optional insurance, most people never think of it until the risk has happened and there is a need. A consumer may have turned down flood insurance and then 3 years later lost his home due to a flood. If he had known that flooding could be an issue, he might have exercised the option to buy the insurance earlier, and certainly looking back, the homeowner likely wishes he had made the purchase.

Establishing security for the applications is the same kind of hindsight situation. It is possible to account for all known threats in the beginning, but it is generally more expensive to do so. Therefore, companies will search for the right balance. Where the issue occurs is when it is not discussed and not made part of the requirements for a project. If security is never discussed and there is a breach, the company is likely to blame the developer. If the issues are discussed and a breach occurs through something left out intentionally, the company has no recourse. It is best to discuss the technical requirement of security up front.

Who Is the Real Customer?

Most PMs feel that the sponsor is the real customer. Although the sponsor is the financial enabler of the project and is generally the ultimate approval authority, the sponsor is not always the real customer. The real customers are the users of the service, application, or product. The reason that this concept is so important is that the sponsor may be so far removed from the actual day-to-day activities that he or she may not be fully qualified to make the decisions. For example, a new company contracted a developer, Michelle, to complete new applications for them. Michelle was assigned to the project and scheduled a meeting to complete the requirements. The scope of the project was to improve the overall speed of the data entry personnel entering the necessary records. The process took roughly 30 minutes per transaction. The project was designed to reduce each entry to 20 minutes or less. Michelle scheduled a meeting to define the requirements. She asked that some of the most senior data entry personnel be included in the requirements definition meetings. Management said that they were too busy and would be unable to attend. Michelle worked with the management team and developed the requirements. Six months later, the new application was revealed to the end users, and they were asked to test the new process. The new application actually made the process worse. It now took almost 45 minutes to complete a transaction. The key reason was that the management team didn't truly understand the process and designed it from their perspective. What was missing was the perspective of the group that was actually completing the transactions and using the application.

It is easy to get confused regarding who the true customer is. The management team was responsible for the ultimate signoff and acceptance of the project—not to mention they signed the check. Their goal was to reduce the overall processing time. In reality, they didn't care how the time frame was reduced, just that the application made it faster per transaction. The mistake was not including the real user: the data entry personnel who would be completing the work.

Sponsors and users should be treated like functional and technical requirements. The "what" and the "how" should be separated. The management team should have identified what they wanted and the success criteria. The users should have been involved in how to make such criteria happen. Do not forget to include the real customer in the requirements definition process.

Work Breakdown Structure Dictionary

One of the key ways to ensure that requirements are clearly identified and met is to ensure that a proper work breakdown structure (WBS) dictionary is utilized. A WBS dictionary takes each element of a defined WBS (described in Chapter 7) and provides detail surrounding the task. A WBS dictionary is usually a form for the project team to fill out for each task. It is normally used in large and complex projects with many moving parts. Although it may seem like quite a bit of work to complete, and it can be, it prevents many of the issues that can occur from miscommunications or a team member misunderstanding what the task is or how it fits into the overall whole of the project. It is a way for a project team to communicate completely what is needed to complete each task. A WBS subdivides each deliverable into smaller manageable pieces for easier estimation. A WBS dictionary takes each piece and defines for the task:

- A unique identifier for each individual task (usually an outline number of the tasks. For instance, if it is the second task to deliver the third deliverable, the number may be 3.2)

- Its name
- A complete description
- Its predecessors and successors
- What the end result should be
- The functional requirement it fulfills
- The technical requirement of completing the task
- Who owns it or should complete it

As teams become geographically and culturally more dispersed, greater communication is necessary. A WBS dictionary facilitates the required communication and makes sure that each team member understands the intent of the task. This step also allows team members to be interchangeable as necessary. When it is time for a task to begin, the PM can send the WBS dictionary to each team member and they should be able to work on it immediately. This step also reinforces the entire chapter. When filling out a WBS dictionary, the PM and team member are faced with describing how the task fits the requirements. The requirements have to fit the scope of the project. This exercise assists in validating requirements and ensuring that the work being done can be tied directly to the scope of the project.

As we discussed in Chapter 5, however, the team members must understand what *done* means. PMs often forget that the end result of the task is also part of the requirements. A great way to ensure the understanding of the task is to ask the team members to describe what the end result will be. This type of confirmation allows everyone to come to the same understanding. Do not accept "yes" or "okay" to confirm the team members' understanding.

DO NOT SACRIFICE YOUR TEAM AT ANY COST!

n the previous chapter, we talked about carefully defining and understanding customer requirements. Once that is done, it is important that your team works together to complete the project. To do so, they must be able to trust their project manager (PM). In this chapter, we discuss why it is so important as the PM to be the champion of your team.

The project management field is riddled with stories and examples of how a project can overburden a team. This overburdening is often caused by a communication failure. Many PMs are afraid to challenge dates or say no and instead sacrifice their teams. This situation promotes an unhealthy work atmosphere and results in disgruntled employees. The most important part of a project is the team doing the work.

Often, the team members will have worked with each other before. It is crucial that the PM ensures that old issues become resolved and focuses on team building. Some PMs are surprised about how much emphasis team building receives when they go through formal training or attend a seminar. Team building is essential in producing quality deliverables in an efficient time frame. Poor project management habits and lack of enforcement of proper planning, on the other hand, hinders the team building experience. In many cases, it can create negative feelings in the team toward management, including the PM. It is the PM's duty to protect and build the team while ensuring satisfaction for them and the customer.

The Importance of the Team Relationship

It is ultimately the team who will complete the work of the project. The team members' cohesiveness, satisfaction, and ability to get the job done are paramount to successful project management. Nevertheless, team management is usually an afterthought for many PMs. The current climate for projects usually means extended hours and stressful situations, often due to a lack of planning or a mandated date. Many project teams are handed a scope of work, time frame, and budget and are asked to execute the project. Yet they are not given a chance to understand the factors and often have no input into the planning whatsoever. This scenario breeds apathy and can be disheartening. The PM needs to understand the importance of the team relationship and how he or she should utilize the team's potential to its fullest. A successful PM will not only recognize the team's value but also will communicate this to the team, so that they are aware that they are valued and respected.

How to Build an Effective Team Relationship

The first step in establishing a relationship with the team is to ask for and listen to their input immediately. Regardless of the information given to the PM at the start of the project, his first action should be to obtain team feedback and input as to the plan's feasibility. Later in the chapter, we will discuss how to deal with a mandated date, but when a project is initially assigned, begin to plan as if the end date is not known. The plan should be centered on the team's ability to understand and complete the deliverables. As we discussed in Chapter 5, feeling "in" on things ranks as one of the highest priorities for an employee. Let the team feel "in" on planning the project and determining the feasibility. This goal is achieved by following the techniques described in Chapter 6, completing a work breakdown structure, activity sequencing, and time estimation. The team building starts when the team is discussing the project tasks and they begin to see how their part fits into the overall whole of the project plan.

Once the team has initial input, the next step is to consistently solicit feedback and offer encouragement to the team. A PM's role is 90 percent about communication, which means constantly checking in with the resources and understanding where they are and what they need to complete their tasks. This is not the usual conversation that most PMs have with their teams. It should not be a typical question of, "What percentage complete is task 122?" Such a question is too broad. There have been many projects that have been 95 percent complete and holding for an entire year. Most team members are hedging bets when they answer such a question. It is almost like a game of "beat the bank." Have you ever accidentally written a check that overdraws your checking account and you quickly deposit the money in your account hoping the check has not been presented? This is sometimes the case when a resource is asked what percentage complete the project is. Afraid to tell the truth, the individual may give a larger figure hoping that he or she can make up the time before the next meeting. This is not an efficient way to ask or receive update information from the team. In addition, the team realizes that most PMs are just plugging this information into a report that will be published. It almost becomes such an automated response that it begins to appear robotic. Instead, ask the team members for updates that require real answers. Ask them engaging questions that are meant to drive a true update, uncover issues, or identify risks. Examples of these questions are:

- How many hours have you worked on this specific task?
- How many hours will it take you to complete the remaining work?

These questions can help uncover a few pieces of information. The PM will be able to establish the percentage complete based on the answers, however, he or she will also be able to determine the level of effort the resource has devoted to the project. If asked how much is done, the resource could say "50 percent." The PM then assumes that if it was a 10-hour task, that 5 hours have been worked. This is the beginning of many miscommunications that can derail the context of the project. Instead, by asking the amount of time worked and the time remaining, the PM can get the same information, but there is more accountability to the question. At any time, a resource can be untruthful in the response, however, it is easier to mislead on a percentage complete question than a level of effort question. Based on how the resource has responded, several follow-up questions can be used:

- We seem to be a bit behind, is there anything that I can do to get you what you need?
- Is there anything that is preventing you from working on or completing the task?
- Did we miss something in the identification of the task?

Based on the response, you can dig up more information from the team member about what issues or risks they may be encountering. In any case, constructive questioning involves the team members more in the conversation. It also engages them in the process of updating the project plan. These techniques can assist in creating a collaborative environment and generate active team conversations that not only provide effective status but also build team relationships. There will be times when the updates are better than expected. This is a great opportunity to show appreciation for the team's hard work and diligence. This positive reinforcement also breeds effective teamwork and encourages other team members to focus on their tasks.

The final step in building an effective team relationship is utilizing a "lessons learned" meeting appropriately. *Lessons learned* are supposed to be a foundation of solid project management, however, many organizations do not find the time or are afraid to hold these sessions. Their fear is that it will become a blame session, hurt team morale, or will not accomplish anything. The reality is that these meetings can be a great way to solidify a team relationship and build a foundation to working more effectively on the next project. The key is to start with positive comments and have a prepared list of what went right. Thank the team members for their accomplishments and truly mean it. Establish ground rules in the beginning of the meeting that state:

- There will be no blame placed for any issues that occurred.
- All things are being discussed to either improve them or avoid a reoccurrence in the future.

- This meeting will not rehash issues, only discuss ways to improve.
- The goal of the meeting is to become better at executing projects.

Establishing the ground rules is important so that if the meeting goes off track, the PM can quickly intercede and keep the team focused on improvement. A "lessons learned" meeting needs to occur and should be used and viewed as a team-building exercise.

■ Internal Team Satisfaction

Team satisfaction should be intertwined in project success criteria. There are many horror stories. One PM had a difficult project that caused the team to burn out, resulting in high turnover. The burnout occurred in trying to hit a specific date. The date was met, but more than 70 percent of the team left, causing a large gap in working knowledge as the end result of the project. It seemed the company was too focused on an arbitrary result than on ensuring team satisfaction. Team building and team satisfaction must be a primary focus for a PM. It is important to celebrate employee accomplishments and continue to reinforce positive team behavior in order to achieve maximum results.

In another example, PM Karen was promoted to project management office manager. In this position, she inherited several PMs with varying skill levels. Her first concern was to make the group a team. They needed to learn to rely on each other's skill sets and knowledge to learn and grow as a team. General motivating factors include prestige, money, and recognition. Karen, however, wanted to establish a level of respect between the team members and use internal recognition as a means of motivation. She instituted a policy at the end of every staff meeting in which each staff member would thank another staff member for assistance that they had received during that week. It was a simple "thank you" policy. In a very short time, the team had taken the exercise and created a game of chance that they played in which the winner would select a team activity, such as bowling or a team lunch for everyone to participate. The team events became bonding events, and within 6 months, the team was a fully functioning and cohesive group. The interesting factor is that because Karen asked the team to thank each other, the group actively sought out things throughout the week that they could discuss during their time to thank the others. This activity made the team focus on searching for positive aspects to discuss instead of those that were negative. When they looked for positive items, they began to see the good in each other and respect each other.

In another organization, the project team leader implemented a positive confrontation policy. This policy was set so that if team members had an issue with each other, they were to deal with it in a private setting. They were to go into a room and discuss the issue and were not to leave until they had reached a better understanding of each other. The premise was that if someone was annoying someone else or something wasn't quite right between two members, it was an issue of understanding each other rather than an issue with each other. The two team members were to emerge from the room with a better understanding of the other person. This method worked in their high-pressure and stressful environment. It gave team members a chance to blow off some steam, yet allowed them to become closer to each other because of it.

Team Building and Conflict Resolution

Internal team satisfaction should be a primary focus for a PM. When a project begins, there must be a strategy regarding how to build the team and to ensure their satisfaction. One of the more popular theorists in the field of satisfaction in the workplace was humanistic psychologist Abraham Maslow (1908–1970). In 1954, Maslow introduced the hierarchy of needs. These appear in a five-stage pyramid, which can be applied in an individual's personal life, as well as in the workplace. The theory is that each stage must be satisfied before the next stage can be achieved. The stages are:

1. **Physiological Needs:** air, food, drink, shelter, warmth, sleep, etc.
2. **Safety Needs:** protection from elements, security, order, law, limits, stability, etc.
3. **Social Needs:** work group, family, affection, relationships, etc.
4. **Esteem Needs:** self-esteem, achievement, mastery, independence, status, dominance, prestige, managerial responsibility, etc.
5. **Self-Actualization:** realizing personal potential, self-fulfillment, seeking personal growth, and peak experiences.

Unless employees' basic physiological and safety needs are met, they can't begin to work on their social needs. PMs generally do not have day-to-day oversight of the team members assigned to their projects. They must rely on influence instead of direct management behavior. Most PMs work in a matrix environment. A matrix environment means that the team members assigned to them report to functional managers that have the human resources responsibilities of dealing with the employees' human needs. Therefore, from a project management perspective, it is difficult to assist an employee in reaching the first two levels of the hierarchy. The PM can exert influence to identify areas of improvement, but it is difficult to directly affect the first two levels.

The third level, social needs, is the primary focus for the PM. Team building and team satisfaction begin at the social needs level. The PM can affect this level by encouraging team interaction and communications. A PM can also be sure to provide ample recognition to the team for their efforts. If a PM can build a cohesive team that meets the social needs of the group, then the team can begin to work toward their esteem needs to eventual self-actualization.

It is difficult to help a resource through the final two levels of the hierarchy (at least in the author's experience), but the movement through the last two levels is a product of momentum. By assisting the functional managers in identifying the gaps in the first two levels and ensuring that the third level is taken care of, the PM has created an environment where the team can ascend through the hierarchy. A focused team in which each person is realizing their personal potential can provide amazing outcomes to project objectives.

◾ 100 Percent/10 Percent Rule

There is a key rule that is controversial in project management. It is the 100 percent/10 percent rule. This rule says:

> As a project manager, I am accountable for 100 percent of the project failure but only 10 percent of the project success.

There are very few PMs that actually believe in this statement, but if this rule is understood and implemented, it can become a powerful tool in team building and career paths. The theory starts with a common idea: pushing a team down versus pulling a team up. If a PM is constantly stepping on the team to try to advance his or her own career or is constantly pushing the team down, eventually, the PM will fall with the team. On the other hand, if a PM is constantly pulling a team up through assistance and positive reinforcement, the PM will naturally move up with the team.

To implement the 100 percent/10 percent rule, the PM must start by assuming 100 percent of the project's failure. This statement means exactly what is implied. Do not allow anyone to blame the team for anything. Assume blame for the failure as the PM. Here are a few examples:

BLAME: The team did a poor job of estimating.

100 PERCENT RESPONSE: I could have done a better job of leading the team through the estimation cycle. Next time, I will be sure to spend more time on this topic.

BLAME: The resource didn't know what he was coding against.

100 PERCENT RESPONSE: I could have done a better job sitting with the resource to ensure that he understood all of the requirements.

BLAME: How can this project be late? Why isn't the team working hard enough?

100 PERCENT RESPONSE: I did not do a good job of setting expectations with you. The team is doing all that they can.

Again, this is a difficult concept for many PMs. There is a simple truth. The PM IS responsible for project success. He or she IS to blame for missing estimates, getting behind schedule, and failing to meet quality requirements. The teachings of Project Management Institute® are leaning this way as well. Poor estimation, unrealistic schedules, and underfunded budgets are a direct result of poor project management. There is a deeper root to this theory. Looking back at Maslow's theories, the 100 percent/10 percent rule protects the team's esteem and ultimately their level one and two needs. If a mistake is made or if a project is derailed, the person responsible could begin to fear for his or her job. Protecting that person from that level of scrutiny can satisfy his or her needs and ensure productivity in the future. A result of the protection is a loyal team member who will look after the PM on the next project. The reverse of the rule is to allow the team member to be sacrificed for the mistake. If the team member is exposed and the PM sacrifices him or her, the PM is sending a message to the rest of the team. This action begins to affect their level three (social) and level two (safety) needs and can result in a loss of productivity.

Some PMs are afraid of using this tactic for fear of their own jobs, however, failure truly is the PM's fault. He or she owns the project, for better or worse. In most cases, it is clear who made the mistake or why a project was derailed. If the PM assumes the responsibility, as should be the case, the respect of the project team is earned. When the project team respects the PM, they will want to ensure success as much as the PM does. This is where the second portion of the rule is applied.

When a project is successful, it is acceptable to celebrate with the team and accept some recognition; however, only 10 percent of the success should be attributable to the PM. When senior management begins to send accolades to the PM, the PM should immediately let it reflect on the team. For instance:

EXECUTIVE: "Tom, you did a great job as project manager on this
   project!"

TOM: "I appreciate that, but it's easy to succeed when you have a team
   like these guys doing all of the heavy lifting! They were so
   motivated, I barely had to show up!"

The statement is true. The team has done most of the work, and the role of the PM is to ensure that it gets done. Make sure the team feels the recognition. The reverse of this rule will breed animosity toward the PM. If you are seen as someone who takes all of the glory, the team will be less likely to perform. Stealing the glory from the team directly violates levels three and four of the hierarchy and will result in an unproductive team for the next project.

▣ How a Team Can Become Overburdened

PMs may find themselves in situations when they are asked to sacrifice their team in order to make a date or a deadline. The question is, what is the significance of a deadline? Is it really necessary to overburden the team to meet a deadline, or is the deadline insignificant? A team can become overburdened by agreeing to a date or an assignment without qualification. The general progression will start with working projects simultaneously and applying extra effort in short bursts. Then, the extra effort becomes the expected result. The final step is that the team becomes completely overburdened.

During the merger of two large banks, a PM named Milo was assigned to the integration and merging of two systems. As the work and demands piled on, Milo found himself continually working more and more hours. To deal with the communication demands, he started coming into the office early. The workday was filled with interruptions and emergencies. The interruptions started taking up the entire day to the point where Milo was unable to complete the planned work for each day. To compensate for the lost time, he would stay late. Before he realized it, his work hours were over 14 hours per day. It was interesting that the work demand never seemed to subside. In fact, Milo felt that he was getting further and further behind. We can become so focused on our daily tasks that it is easy to overburden ourselves. It takes willpower not to overcommit to impending deadlines. Is this the quality of life that the PM wanted? It's very doubtful that anyone wants to work 14-hour days and not feel like he or she is accomplishing anything. For Milo, it was his decision to begin to work longer hours.

The PM must also realize that his or her decisions can easily overburden a team as well. As easily as Milo was overburdened, it can be even easier to overburden the team. The PM must understand this concept.

A team can become overburdened for a variety of reasons. The most common reasons are that the corporate sponsor:

- Does not understand the utilization of the team (this will be discussed in detail in Chapter 14)
- Fails to understand the other demands on the team
- Adheres to mandated dates without qualification

The last two bullet points are the most common. They are errors of misunderstanding. The next two sections will cover areas that are conveyed by failures to communicate. Meaning, it is human nature to assume what the other person knows. In the cases of understanding demands and blind acceptance of mandated dates, the results are overburdened teams.

■ Interacting with Requestors to Avoid Overburdening

Sponsors and stakeholders often request work, new projects, and assign tasks throughout their day-to-day routine. The first assumption that can overburden a team is that the sponsor is aware of all of the demands on the team. If a PM just accepts each new task or project without qualification, then the sponsor or stakeholder is going to assume that the work is going to get done. If the PM never challenges the request or amount of requests, then the sponsor or stakeholder will assume that the team has the capacity. As discussed, the best way to manage a project is to listen to a request, assess the impact, and then present options to the requestor. This process is utilized here as well. When a sponsor or stakeholder asks that something be completed, the PM should assess the request and tell the requestor about the impact on the team. For example, an executive witnessed an inefficient process being completed by one of his employees. He contacted a PM named Max and requested a project that would identify the cause of the inefficiencies, utilize technology to automate the process, and publish the end results. At the end, the following conversation occurred:

Executive (Exec): "When do you think that can be completed?"

Max (PM): "We can get it completed by November."

Exec: "November? It is only February."

PM: "Yes sir. There are four projects that are in front of this one. They are (a list of four projects). We could put this one before one of those, hire an outside firm to complete this one, or complete it as soon as we can, which right now is projected to be November."

Exec: "I don't have the budget for an outside firm, and the four projects are all high-priority projects. I guess I will have to live with November."

PM: "If any of the other projects can be completed sooner, then we will get on this one immediately."

Exec: "Fair enough."

If Max had not challenged the date, then he would have overcommitted his team. There will be times when it is unavoidable to overcommit the team, but this should only happen in circumstances that absolutely warrant it. The typical response to this type of conversation is to agree with the stakeholder without qualification and ask the team to double up their work to complete the project. This choice creates two problems. First, because there was no qualification and no discussion, the sponsor assumes the team has the capacity and will complete the project. The second issue is that the team will have to work twice as hard and in the end hope for some recognition for their efforts. This acknowledgment doesn't come, however, because the sponsor is unaware of the extra effort needed to complete the project. The sponsor is unaware because the PM who accepted the work didn't qualify and quantify the project request.

If it appears that the team is about to become overburdened, another effective way to assist in task prioritization is to create a list of all demands on the team. Then, ask the senior manager, sponsor, or executive committee to prioritize the list. This type of organization at least makes the leadership aware of the demand on the team. Hopefully, the end result is an understanding reached by the executive in the dialogue just used as an example. An understanding of what can and can't be completed and an understanding of the demand can prevent overburdening a team.

▒ Dealing with Mandated Dates

A mandated date is the pitfall of many a project. It can be one of the most common reasons work can fail because date itself is not usually qualified. The first mistake many PMs make is announcing the mandated date at the beginning of the project estimation process. Their opening statement is, "This project has to be done by June 30, now when do you think you can complete this project?" Should the PM be surprised if the answer is June 30? It is like supplying the answers to a test and then administering the test. It is preconditioning the team to a specific response. As a PM, it is important to understand if the mandated date is a realistic date. To do this, follow the Program Evaluation Review Technique (PERT) process discussed in Chapter 7. Identify the activities, find the critical path, and then let the date "fall out" of the plan. Do not ask the team, "When will you be done?" Ask, "What needs to be completed before you can start your task, and how long will it take you to complete this task?" Even better, make sure the resource provides a best-case, a most-likely, and a worst-case estimate by task.

Use a scheduling tool like Microsoft Project or Open Workbench. Let the date tool compute the end date of the project; this will be the first pass at a true completion date. When setting up a plan in a project tool, follow these main rules:

Rule 1: All tasks except for the very first one should have a predecessor assigned.

Reason: The plan needs to be dynamic. If a task is late, how does it affect the plan? If a task is early, what should be worked on next? If the plan is not reacting dynamically, then the power of a scheduling tool is lost.

Rule 2: Do not manually enter dates.

Reason: Durations and relationships can control the schedule. It may seem difficult to learn the scheduling tool, but invest the time. It will save a tremendous amount of time later.

Rule 3: Define the durations.

Reason: As stated in rule two, the schedule must be controlled by relationships and durations. Defining the durations ensures that each task has been identified and understood. This is an important step in letting the date fall.

Rule 4: Always baseline your plan.

Reason: This step has several reasons. First, the plan must always be baselined in order to be able to measure against it. It is also possible to save multiple baselines. The first baseline should be the original plan. The other baselines can be after significant events such as a scope change or to track changes (the changes in a plan will be shown versus the baseline). This step will also reap benefits discussed in Chapter 12. In order to know if the project is ahead or behind schedule, it must be compared to the baseline.

Rule 5: Update the plan regularly!

Reason: A plan is dynamic. It must be updated to truly be managed. Make sure there are no past due start or finish dates on the plan.

Once the plan is set up properly and the information is entered, the date will fall out. In most cases, the date that the plan falls on is later than the requested date. There are three common situations in which this happens.

Case 1: Improper or extremely conservative estimations by the team. Before negotiations begin with the sponsor, make sure that your estimates are not too conservative. Make sure that the plan is sound and that it does reflect reality. If more time or more resources are requested and the plan is overflowing with risk days, the negotiation will stop there.

Case 2: The projected date is the requested date. In this case, work with the sponsor to negotiate a completion. One technique is to take all of the risk out of the plan and determine the date (putting risk into a plan is discussed in Chapter 12). Then, have a range of dates to take to the sponsor. In the delivery of the message, state that if everything goes as planned, the project will come in on this date. The worst-case scenario projections will bring the project in on another date. Although this sounds like a simplistic approach, it is really quite powerful. You're not saying that the team can't complete the project on the date specified. You are simply saying that the projections, according to the plan, show the project falling between these two dates. Wait for the sponsor's reaction and adjust appropriately. If the sponsor says it has to be done within a shorter time frame, then the PM can request additional resources. Often, the sponsor will accept the range that was given. React to the sponsor's answer, but have a few suggestions ready. Of course, there will be times when the sponsor will reject the estimates and demand the time frame originally requested. In this case, manage the team as best as you can to meet that deadline, but do not change the dates on the project plan. Let the plan reflect reality and have it land on the date that the team has estimated. This will be your primary communication tool.

Case 3: The requested end date is a regulatory or mandated date and can't be moved without repercussions. This is a difficult case but not impossible. Generally, when an aggressive date is given, the schedule becomes compressed in the final stages of the project. This schedule change usually happens because the team has not modified their approach to the project and time is running out. Therefore, they sacrifice or compress whatever tasks remain (generally testing or training). If the plan is set up early and is truly dynamic, then it is easier to find where to compress your schedule.

For example, Val was the PM working for an extremely risk-adverse company when it came to the implementation of new technology. She was given a project that had a completion date of June 30 established by a governing agency. When she laid out the project plan using the standard process and the standard time frames, the project completion date showed the middle of September. Many PMs would not find out this constraint until later in the project because they didn't set up the plan properly or they used manually adjusted estimates to meet June 30. When using tailored estimates, the team will not generally fall really behind schedule until the middle or end of the project. Then, the team has to scramble, usually sacrificing testing and/or quality in the process, to finish the project.

Using the project plan, the team started to work out different scenarios to crash the schedule and bring the date to the regulatory deadline. They worked out the scenarios by changing different estimates and viewing the reaction of the plan. This method takes trial and error, but is well worth the effort. The team noticed that the hardware delivery, building, and configuration were areas that they thought could be improved. They did not want to sacrifice any testing, quality, or training activities. The team then continued to move the dates involving the hardware until the project plan fell into place. This schedule change gave Val a "drop dead" date for the hardware while keeping the rest of the plan intact. With this information, she went to the sponsor and said that the current projections are estimating the end date of the project in the middle of September. If the sponsor would commit to some additional cost, however, the team could overnight the hardware and purchase an accelerated build process. If the team could guarantee the hardware would be ready by mid-February, then the project had a better-than-average chance to meet the June 30th date. If the sponsor did not allow the extra cost, there was a good chance they would miss the date. The end result was adding the additional cost, and the project was finished 2 weeks earlier than the June 30th date.

The lesson of this example is that a properly set project plan (following the rules in this chapter) saved this company from a number of common outcomes:

- A regulatory fine due to not completing the project on time
- A poor-quality implementation by compressing the tasks at the end of a project (which are usually quality, testing, or training)
- An overburdened team

Using proper project management techniques, creating a solid project plan, and quantifying and qualifying desired dates are keys to ensuring that a team is not sacrificed. Happy teams produce great products. Great products ensure customer satisfaction. Customer satisfaction ensures longevity in business. Do not sacrifice your team at any cost, because the cost of sacrificing the team can't be measured.

MYTHS ABOUT STATUS MEETINGS

n the previous chapter, we talked about the importance of protecting and respecting your team. One of the most common interactions you will have with your team will be at status meetings. Learning how to make these meetings effective and useful is an important part of becoming a successful project manager (PM).

Most of your day as a PM likely consists of meetings. Everything in the world seemingly has to be communicated in a meeting. Frankly, this is an extremely large waste of time. It breeds complacency and hurts productivity. Meetings are inevitable, but having some general rules in place can streamline meetings and make them helpful rather than harmful. In this chapter, we discuss the function of a meeting, when to call one and when not to, and how to make them effective. We also discuss the general rules for holding fantastic meetings, as well as some myths about status meetings.

▪ Understanding the Purpose of Meetings

According to www.dictionary.com, the word *meeting* means, "the act of coming together." There is also another meaning. That is, "a hostile encounter." PMs have encountered both. The corporate world tends to abuse them. As one consultant said, "If you want to kill an afternoon, call a meeting." This type of attitude stops meetings from being productive. Another consultant said, "I call my meetings at 7 minutes past the start of the hour because people are always running late." When asked, "Do people make it on time now?" he said they didn't. If people feel so negatively, why are there so many meetings?

The first reason is that people feel obligated to hold meetings. There is a myth that because a project exists, a status meeting must exist. The problem with this thinking is that it conditions people to not be productive during the week. The project can fall quickly into a routine. When a resource comes into work on status meeting day, she quickly sees that there is a meeting to discuss her progress for the past week. She hurriedly looks over the notes sent from the last meeting (because she forgot what she was supposed to do) and works on the assigned task or issue. Then at the meeting, she can report progress. After the conclusion of the meeting, she forgets about the next steps and goes about her day. This example is not meant as a dig at the resource. She can't remember all of her tasks because she is on multiple projects and has multiple meetings.

The same can be said for PMs running multiple projects. Sometimes, they forget to do their follow-up until they are creating the agenda for the next meeting. For example, a PM is looking over his calendar and sees that he needs to create an agenda for the next one. Then, the PM looks over the notes from the previous status meeting and realizes that he forgot to follow up on a couple of items and quickly sends out e-mails to try to rectify the issue.

Most likely, the PM and the resources are in so many meetings, it is hard to get any actual work done. Meetings are where people generally come to talk about the things that they need to do. The problem is that if there are more meeting hours than work hours in a day, less tasks are actually accomplished. People feel obligated to have a status meeting; they feel obligated to have a meeting to discuss a decision, bring up an issue, or deal with a particular problem. Somehow, having a meeting has come to be a sign of progress in our corporate culture.

We are not suggesting that you not have status meetings or not hold meetings at all. They are a necessary part of business, but there are rules for having good meetings, and there are ways to make them useful and productive, rather than just a waste of time. There are situations that warrant meetings and situations that do not. Understanding the differences and using them effectively are ways to increase the project team's productivity.

▓ Should There Be a Meeting?

There are some simple questions you should ask yourself before calling a meeting.

- **Is there anything to say?** One of the worst kinds of status meetings to attend is the type in which everyone goes around the room and states what they accomplished the prior week. This practice is a colossal waste of time. An effective PM can get these updates prior to a meeting, distribute them, and then discuss issues at the meeting. Going around the room and asking what was accomplished is a waste of everyone's time. If this is the entire point of the meeting, then don't call one.
- **Does there have to be a meeting?** Some PMs will call a team meeting to resolve an issue between two team members. Others call meetings to come up with options for a decision that the team does not have the power to make. If the issue can be handled with a conference call, e-mails, or individually face-to-face, do not call a meeting!
- **Do we have input?** Have you ever been to a meeting to discuss a decision or an issue when the decision was already made? Why did that meeting even need to be called? If a decision is made or that input from the team is not really needed, then do not call the meeting. Calling a meeting to have the team hear the rationale for a decision that is already made will do more damage than just announcing the decision. Calling the meeting will waste their time and will hurt team morale. The time for input is before a decision. Once a decision is made, input is not useful.
- **Do we have to escalate?** This type of meeting is most common when an e-mail war breaks out and everyone starts getting

copied. Generally it is a disagreement between two individuals. Then, the individuals begin to copy their boss for protection. Then more and more inflammatory e-mails go out, and now a meeting must be called to get to the bottom of the issue. If this is occurring on the project, stop it there. Get the two individuals to calm down and discuss the issue. If the problem is still complex enough to call a meeting, then do so, but only call it after both parties have calmed down, tried to resolve the conflict again on their own, and cannot resolve it.

If the meeting requires the team's input, can't be handled via conference call, and has a planned deliverable or outcome, then call the meeting. Otherwise, respect the team's time and allow them to accomplish their work.

▪ Are Your Meetings Effective?

There was a recent survey done at 3M asking team members their thoughts on meetings. The survey showed that the reasons team members did not attend meetings were:

- No decisions were made
- People were not prepared
- Meetings don't stay on the agenda
- Meetings don't start and end on time
- Meetings lasted too long
- Meetings were not well run
- There was no agenda or focus
- There were no or inaccurate notes
- Unnecessary for me to attend

The survey results turn right into a checklist of how to run effective meetings. Use this list to help you avoid the biggest meeting pitfalls.

There can be many signs that meetings are ineffective. The first sign is the respect (or lack thereof) that the team exhibits during status meetings. Are they on time? Are they leaving early? What is their behavior during the meeting? Answering these questions can assist in understanding whether the team is seeing value in the meetings. For instance, if they are consistently showing up late or leaving early, what is that saying about the content of the meeting? It is unlikely that the individuals would show the same disrespect to their bosses or executives in their meetings.

The PM's common initial reaction to this type of disrespect for meetings is normally one of contempt for the team member, although she may not be the problem. Maybe the meeting isn't important enough or doesn't accomplish enough to warrant the team's attention. If a team member is frequently missing or leaving a meeting, ask the resource why she is doing this. Try to understand what is driving the resource to not be on time. You can't assume that this behavior is on purpose. There are many factors that could cause the individual to be late such as other meetings, commitments, or scheduling conflicts. The question that needs to be answered is whether or not the meeting itself is the issue. If the meeting is not warranting the attention of the resources, then either make it worth their while or discontinue the meetings.

Another sign of an ineffective meeting is whether anything was accomplished since the prior meeting. If the resources are consistently stating that no progress was made on their tasks or that after an hour, there are very few action items or deliverables, then the meeting's worth is questionable. PM Perez was was leading a development project and held weekly status meetings to report on the progress of the project and visually show the team the product as it was being created. A significant change request was rendered, and it was estimated it would take the team roughly 6 weeks to complete the work. The first 4 weeks would consist of working on the visual aspects of the product, and therefore, it would be unavailable for viewing during that time. The development PM requested a hiatus on status meetings until the product was viewable. The client PM insisted that they still meet. The next 4 weeks consisted of everyone dialing into a conference call, signing into a desktop-sharing application, and doing or showing absolutely nothing. There was no reason to meet. The development team was working on the viewable portion, and it would be at least 4 weeks to complete. Perez should have recognized the lack of information and canceled the meetings. At the very least, he could have asked just the development PM to attend a meeting and provide updates, issues, or questions. Both the client team and the development team should have been allowed to continue working without the interruption of the status meeting.

Another sign of an ineffective meeting is when a PM is forcing an update or is trying to show up one of the resources that is not completing her tasks. This action forces untruthful behavior and is bullying the resource. A resource told about a PM who would bully a resource until she gave the update or stated what the PM wanted to hear. This kind of behavior is a disservice to the resource, the PM, and the entire project team. This conduct only breeds animosity, and pushing for information that is not there can lead to project disaster. The PM would report what she eventually heard in the meeting and then when the project would be behind or off track, would blame the resource and hang him or her out to dry. If people are being forced to be untruthful, suffice it to say that the meeting is ineffective.

Setting Up a Successful Meeting

There are some general guidelines to follow in order to have successful and effective meetings.

IDENTIFY THE OBJECTIVE

Follow the qualification steps discussed earlier in this chapter to determine if the meeting is necessary. Determine what the outcome of the meeting is supposed to be and state it on the meeting invitation. Instead of a generic meeting title, choose one that is more descriptive. For example, change "Conversion Project Team Meeting" to "Decision on Software Platform (Conversion Project)." Identify what the meeting will cover and its desired outcome.

SCHEDULE TIME AND STICK TO IT

Choose a start and stop time and ensure that the meeting adheres to those times. If the meeting is going to run over, schedule the next one or give the team an opportunity to make the decision to run over. Not releasing the resources on time and failing to adhere to the schedule sets a poor example for the project team. How can a PM expect that the resources will hit their estimates if the PM can't hit his?

CREATE AN AGENDA

Not only should the PM create an agenda, she should also assign topic owners, avoid acronyms, and set expected times for the topics. Ray, a senior PM consultant was asked to attend a meeting that was titled "CRM Discussion" where he was assigned the task "CRM Overview." He assumed that CRM meant customer relationship management and that he would be providing an overview of the concept. There were no attendees listed, so he assumed that it was an internal meeting. When Ray arrived at the meeting, he realized that he was the only one dressed in business casual. He also noticed clients in the room and a projector set up. The slide on the projector said "Change Request Management Demonstration" and had Ray's name next to it. He was completely unprepared. Granted, Ray made way too many assumptions, however, the meeting agenda and title were not sufficient. The agenda should include:

- The start and stop times of the meeting
- The goal of the meeting
- A list of participants
- The roles and responsibilities of the participants
- The location of the meeting
- Special considerations such as dress code, directions, or information that is pertinent to the outcome of the meeting
- Definitions of all acronyms used

ENSURE THE ATTENDEES ARE PREPARED

It is the PM's role to ensure that all attendees understand why they are there, what is expected of them, and what their attendance means to the project. This exercise has two different purposes. When a PM is gathering the information to tell the resources why they are needed, the PM is validating that they are needed. The second purpose is to ensure that the participant brings the necessary materials and/or mindset to have a successful meeting.

Successful meetings can really be quite simple. It is amazing the productivity that can be achieved by following these rules. Not only will the productivity level go up, but word of mouth on how the meetings are run will get around as well. Success can also hinge on the preconception of the meeting. If a resource walks in thinking the meeting will be a waste of time, most likely it will. On the other hand, if the resource understands why he or she is needed, has time to prepare for the discussions or tasks at hand, and knows what the desired outcome is of the meeting, then he or she is more likely to accomplish the objective.

Important Rules for Meetings

TIMELINESS

One of the first and most important rules of meetings is to not let meetings drag on. One project office manager once discussed a staff meeting that would take 2.5 hours with four people attending. His input was about 20 minutes. The time lost over the other two-plus hours was an incredible blow to his productivity. Make sure that the meetings are efficient.

HOLD TO THE PURPOSE OF THE MEETING

Do not allow other topics or political issues to cloud the meeting. Call another meeting to discuss the latest issue or agree to talk about it after the original meeting task is completed.

ENSURE THAT ALL NEEDED MATERIALS ARE PRESENT

Make sure that all information needed to achieve the outcome is available. If the meeting is to discuss a user interface, then make sure the interface is available for viewing. If it is a meeting to choose one vendor over another, make sure that appropriate information is available to make the decision.

DOCUMENT ALL DETAILS AND DECISIONS

If the meeting is important enough to bring together a team, it needs to be documented. The meeting can either be documented in meeting minutes (a formal listing all conversation) or meeting notes (which are less formal and do not contain everything everyone said). Meeting notes list the key decisions and who took part in the conversation but not at the same detailed level as meeting minutes. Whichever the case, make sure the key points are documented.

How to Get a Meeting Back on Track

There are a couple of tactics that a PM can use to bring a meeting back on track once it has started to derail. The PM can suggest a follow-up or outside meeting and to discuss the current time and agenda. You can suggest that you take an issue or discussion "off-line," which means to discuss it outside of the meeting. People commonly say, "Let's take that off-line." You can use this term to quickly end a conversation that is derailing a project meeting. If the meeting agenda is to discuss a particular issue and then a new issue arises that commands the conversation, suggesting a follow-up meeting or taking the meeting off-line is a great way to refocus the team. This type of derailment occurs often when stakeholders or sponsors are attending the meeting. They will begin to discuss something that has just occurred or a new "hot button," and the meeting goes off track. Do not be afraid to suggest another time to talk about the issue. It is not a rude suggestion, and when handled properly, it can earn you respect. Often, derailed conversations do not require the input of the present team. Allowing the conversation to continue unabated will begin to waste the team's time and cause a loss of productivity. Side conversations are inevitable and sometimes can create great value for the project. The key is to not let the side conversation go on too long.

Another tactic is to provide a checkpoint during the meeting to check on the progress of the meeting. For example, "Thank you for that discussion. All right, we are on agenda item four of nine and we have 35 minutes left to discuss them." It is a nice subtle suggestion about how fast or slow things are progressing in the meeting. Often, it is met with, "You're right, let's get going." Again, side conversations and meeting derailment are inevitable, however, this tactic shows the team that the PM is cognizant of the time and resets the expectation that the agenda will be followed and completed.

It takes practice and tact to bring a meeting back in line. One question commonly asked about these approaches is, "How do I know when a side conversation has gone too long?" Look at the body language and the facial expressions of the team to help determine when to step in. If two people are engaged in a discussion and the other 10 people are looking around the room, doodling on their pads, or staring in the distance, it is time to step in. A meeting is definitely a place where the majority should rule. If the larger group is not interested in the conversation, it is time to move on. There will be cases when the side conversationalists will insist on completing the conversation. In these cases, suggest that it happens at the end of the meeting after most of the people can be released.

A Big Meeting Faux Pas and Myth

A meeting faux pas that is carried out too often is the sponsor reset. This occurs when a status meeting has started and updates are being provided. Then, the sponsor comes in late (sometimes as much as 30 minutes) and the PM will essentially start the meeting over. He will recap all of the items discussed, ask for comments, and rehash everything that has already happened for the sponsor's benefit. This is a faux pas because it is a subtle, but huge statement to the team that the sponsor is so important that everyone else has to hear everything already said once again. When any other team member comes in late to a meeting, does the PM restart the meeting? Usually the answer is no.

It is acceptable to tell the sponsor where on the agenda the team is as well as answer questions about items already discussed, but do not recap the whole meeting. Leah was a PM who had a reputation for sponsor resets. She was so focused on ensuring that the sponsor approved of the way she was running the project, she could not wait to explain everything when the sponsor eventually came to the meeting. The sponsor had several high-priority projects, and her time was quite thin, so arriving late was often the case. The project team became so frustrated at the meeting restarts that they asked nothing unless the sponsor was present.

Simple actions like restarting the meeting can condition a team. Because sponsors generally provide the financial backing for a project, they are quite important, however, so is the team doing the work. The PM needs to ensure successful and productive encounters. This means starting and stopping on time, even if the sponsor is late and misses part of the meeting.

The myth involved in this situation is that the sponsor wants to hear all information, which is not always the case. One sponsor actually said that she consistently arrives to status meetings 30 to 45 minutes late. It is not a sign of disrespect. It is a way that she maximizes her time. She was not interested in the reporting of accomplishments, hearing all of the issues and listening to the debates. She did not feel this was productive for her. She did want to attend, however, so that any decisions that were deferred to her in the first part of the meeting could be made, she could deal with escalated issues, and she could get the general feeling of the team morale and project progress. A PM who would restart a meeting when she arrived would be counterproductive to her as well. As always, it is a case-by-case decision because there are times when a restart is necessary, however, it should not be automatic.

The Team Morale Killer

We explained earlier in the chapter that status meetings that go around the room and have everyone update their progress are a waste of time. These can also be morale killers. By bringing up everything that was accomplished the prior week, the team is likely to rehash issues that have already been closed. In project management and human resources classes, they teach about conflict resolution techniques. A couple of those methods are smoothing and compromising. Smoothing points out the areas in a disagreement that the parties agree on. In a compromise, each party gives up something to reach middle ground. This is not a chapter on conflict resolution, but we touch on this topic because when the techniques have already been applied, it is best to move forward. Having a meeting that rehashes old issues will likely undo any of the conflict resolution already completed.

Keep the meeting focused on the current issues and tasks. Do not allow the meeting to get turn a finger-pointing session or rehash issues that have been solved. This type of conflict in a project meeting will kill the team's morale.

How to Close a Meeting Successfully

Once the meeting has met the objective listed, it is time to adjourn the meeting. The closing is a very important step. It is not acceptable to just reach the end of the agenda and then thank the team and release them.

The final step of the meeting is to recap the meeting's key points and ensure that the team has consensus. The following items should be discussed in the meeting closing.

KEY TEAM DECISIONS

A quick recap of the decisions made in the meeting.

ACTION ITEMS WITH DUE DATES

Announce the action item captured, who it belongs to, and the target resolution date. It is important to capture the target resolution date to ensure that the action item's sense of urgency is relayed.

KEY TOPIC FOLLOW-UP ASSIGNMENTS

Outside of action items, generally more research is needed to reach consensus on certain decisions. Make sure that the owner of that issue knows that he will be required to lead that topic discussion in the next meeting.

ANNOUNCE SIDE MEETINGS

If an off-line meeting has been requested or is necessary, make sure that all off-line topics are assigned. Review when the off-line meeting will be held and who will be attending.

SET UP THE NEXT MEETING

If possible, confirm the time and date of the next meeting.

CLOSE THE MEETING WITH A TIME CHECK

If the meeting was scheduled for an hour and it took 45 minutes, acknowledge it. State, "We had an hour scheduled, and due to your preparedness, we only needed 45 minutes, enjoy your 15 minutes of found time." If the meeting ran late, apologize to the team and ensure that it won't happen again. This last step proves to the team that the PM understands that their time is valuable and that he appreciates the time received.

ALWAYS, ALWAYS THANK THE TEAM

The last statement should always be a sincere thank you to the team for their time and efforts.

The final step to close the meeting is to document all of the items previously listed and distribute them to the team. Remember to keep this timely, as meeting notes are generally geared toward the people that could not attend the meeting. In addition, expediting the meeting documentation will assist in reminding the team of what needs to be done.

Knowing how to make meeting relevant and useful is an important skill; however, even the most carefully planned meeting can be derailed by unexpected demands or attacks. In the next chapter, we will talk about how to handle those kinds of problems.

PATRIOTS AND SCUDS

According to www.wikipedia.com, the definition of a Scud is "the popularized term for a series of tactical ballistic missiles developed by the Soviet Union during the Cold War and exported widely to other countries." This missile was modified by the Iraqis for use in the Persian Gulf War and was used to attack U.S. forces. A Patriot, as defined by www.army-technology.com is "a long-range, all-altitude, all-weather air defense system to counter tactical ballistic missiles, cruise missiles, and advanced aircraft." Patriots were used in the Persian Gulf War to intercept Scuds and prevent them from doing damage.

Dealing with Patriots and Scuds

What do Patriots and Scuds have to do with project management? Let's first explore the Scud. Helena was a consultant who was on an extended support contract for a client. She reported to the site as if she were employed by the client and managed the day-to-day activities of a computer support operation. As part of her position, she was involved in several status, planning, and support meetings. On one particular day, she passed one of her project stakeholders two or three different times in the hallways. Each time, they made small talk asking how each other was and how the families were doing, etc. The conversations were friendly. That afternoon, in a project meeting, the stakeholder "threw Helena under the bus" in front of roughly 20 people. The stakeholder acted appalled at the project team performance and blew an issue well out of proportion, without ever having mentioned this to the PM before as a concern.

Helena was extremely frustrated. The issue that was brought up had happened several days before, and the stakeholder had had ample opportunity to resolve this situation with her personally before the meeting. The stakeholder, however, decided to wait for the largest venue and drop a bomb, a.k.a. SCUD!

When she began to explore and analyze the situation, she discovered that the stakeholder was behind in her project deliverables and decided to divert attention to the project manager's (PM's) team. Once the consultant realized this, she sought out one of her mentors for advice. This is where the Patriot comes in.

Following her mentor's advice, about 2 hours before the next status meeting, Helena stopped by the stakeholder's desk. She asked, "Is there anything that I can do for you or any issues I need to resolve?" The answer was, "No, I think we have everything handled." That afternoon in the meeting, once again the stakeholder launched a Scud, similar to the one used at the earlier meeting. Then Helena launched her Patriot. "Ms. Stakeholder, I was just in your office about 2 hours ago and specifically asked if you had any concerns, and you didn't bring this up then. Did you just remember this issue in the meeting?"

You could hear a pin drop in the meeting. The stakeholder was a bit embarrassed and did not know how to respond. Helena then followed up with, "We can take this off-line and resolve it after the meeting if that is acceptable to you." The stakeholder willingly agreed. After 2 or 3 weeks of the cold shoulder, they were able to handle their issues off-line and outside of the team meeting. The use of the Patriot not only deflected the current Scud, but it also prevented future Scuds.

Because she was a consultant, Helena had to stand up for herself in that situation. Many times, if you are an internal employee, you may not have the ability to make such a statement in the meeting. Maybe the person launching Scuds is a higher-level manager or your direct superior. In this case, still hold the "Patriot Meeting." If someone is consistently calling you out in a meeting, seek him or her out before the meeting and see if you can destroy the Scud before it lands.

The Patriots and Scuds analogy fits completely to the end. In a war, a Scud and a Patriot neutralize each other, but they both cost money to manufacture, require people to operate them, and if either misses the mark, they can do quite a bit of damage. This is true for meetings as well. A Scud launcher generally is trying to divert attention from him- or herself or is trying to make you look bad in front of the group. If the person misfires, it can look like a malicious attack. The same applies to the Patriot launcher—if you don't fire it correctly, it can cause collateral damage to the stakeholder, which may reflect back upon you and your project.

■ Understand Your Own Missiles

Now ask yourself this uncomfortable question: Are you a Scud launcher or a Patriot launcher? Look back at any recent conflicts you were involved in. Did you launch a Scud? Did you misfire a Patriot? The best approach is to handle conflict in a one-on-one situation as much as possible and make sure you are dealing with the issue, not the person.

Many times, in the heat of a moment, you make assumptions that the person is the issue. "Carol's tasks are always late," or "John never takes my suggestions." The truth is that we relate issues to personality faults or assume that the people are doing it on purpose. Often, this is not the case. If a meeting with Carol starts with "We are here to discuss why you can't complete your tasks on time," most likely it will be an unproductive meeting. If instead you say, "Carol, I need to figure out how to get you more information or better instructions. On your last 10 tasks, you have missed your deadline on all of them. What can I do to help you meet your next 10?" you present the same message, but direct it to the issue, missing tasks, and not the person.

If, however, you are unable to resolve the situation, then protect yourself. Wait for the launch, fire the Patriot, and blast the Scud out of the sky!

▓ Understanding Missiles

If you really start to think about this topic, you will realize that Patriots and Scuds are just as strategic as the battles in which they are used. They each have their own functions and uses. There are certain situations in which each is most appropriate and most effective.

In military conflicts, a Scud is launched to achieve an objective. It is a proactive weapon, one that is used to prevent something from happening or to stop a situation in progress. In many ways, it is an offensive weapon that is launched without a previous attack.

A Patriot is launched to diffuse the perceived threat to the objective. This is not just a technique to deflect intended harm to you or your project objectives. A Patriot is a defensive weapon, one that is used once a threat is already in place. Patriots and Scuds are launched for several other reasons.

▓ Using Patriots

You may decide to launch a Patriot to ease a quickly escalating conflict in a meeting. One of the greatest examples of this is the extremely common phrase, "Let's take this off-line." This one is normally launched to diffuse the constant barrage of Scuds being launched between two parties. For example, a vendor and a business manager could be at odds with each other as to why a task is overdue. They both begin to launch Scuds at each other trying to affix blame on one another. You as the PM could launch the Patriot suggesting a not-so-public "off-line" meeting to resolve the issues. This get-together will hopefully cause a cease-fire between the two parties ending any further damage to the relationship.

▓ Using Scuds

You may decide to launch a Scud to protect your team or a team member from unnecessary abuse. The team could be under constant duress from another team or team leader. Although you may have let a few Scuds past your defenses, there is a point where it crosses the line for your liking. At that point, you launch a Scud back to return the teams to a level playing field. Tim was managing a software development team and had been working diligently on a project that appeared to have delays. He knows that the delays are due to many changes brought on by the team leader, but these changes have not made it to the team leader's boss. Meeting after meeting, the team leader complains of delays and the time it is taking to develop the application. Tim has endured these complaints not wanting to upset the team leader whose participation he needs to complete the project. The team leader, however, has launched yet another Scud in front of his boss, saying that he doesn't understand why the project is not completed. This is not a time for a Patriot. This is a time for a retaliatory Scud. Tim announces that the delays are due to the ever-changing requirements and he outlines the delays incurred. The team leader is now left to explain his actions to his boss.

In this example, you may wonder why Tim let so many Scuds land before firing back. This is a common question. The main reason is that although Patriots and Scuds have their purpose, you do not want to just fire them for the sake of firing them. Just as in battle, they must be a measured response. Contract negotiations are often a litany of Scuds and Patriots. In the end, a compromise should be drawn up; many times, it should truly be a treaty.

■ Missiles in Public

Throughout this chapter, we have talked about Patriots and Scuds in terms of public meetings. Although Scuds are generally public, Patriots do not always have to be. Jack was a consultant working on a project that had to validate that items met a specific validation criteria. To make the process easier, a software test was created to be run at every corporate server, and the results were reported. Based on the results, each server administrator would need to perform a series of actions to bring the server up to code. Out of all of the servers Jack ran the test on, only three servers failed to be up to specifications. He notified the server administrator and prepared for the status meeting. At the status meeting, he reported the results. Then, the server administrator fired his Scud. He announced that he had written a program that could discredit the software test being used by the consultant. The server administrator went on to launch several other Scuds announcing his experience at several other companies around town to bolster his own ego. Instead of simply applying the requested patches to the server, the server administrator took it personally and tried to discredit the consultant. Jack allowed the Scud to land and continued the status meeting.

Prior to the next status meeting, Jack launched his Patriot. He had called the other organizations to find out that the server administrator had indeed worked for the other companies. Using his connections, Jack also found out that the server administrator had been let go from all of the other organizations for poor performance. Instead of making an embarrassing revelation in front of the whole group and possibly causing overall strain on him and his client, Jack approached the server administrator directly. He revealed the information that he had learned, asked him to refrain from making inflammatory remarks in the status meeting, and to apply the updates to the servers. At the next status meeting, the only words uttered by the server administrator were, "The updates have been applied to the three servers, and the tests were rerun to validate the environment."

■ Missiles in Corporate Culture

It is important to understand that corporate politics and culture go way beyond right and wrong. Everyone's point of view is different. Every corporate culture is different.

There are organizations that have been built by seeing who could launch the biggest Scud. And there are organizations where people sit around coming up with terrific Patriots to use to protect themselves. Each person has to assess his or her own company's tone and approach.

Just like in military conflicts, those who research, identify, react, adjust, and monitor are those that come out on top. Whether you decide to launch a Patriot or Scud, make sure you have thought through the next few steps to try to anticipate the reactions. You need to understand how your missile will be received and how the recipient will respond. Different missiles work best in different situations.

■ Always Have an Escape Strategy

It is important to make sure that you do not take too strong of a position in a meeting. There should always be room for a misunderstanding. For example, PM Lin was working with a consultant named George on a project. George had provided time estimates to Lin for a particular task. Lin was familiar with the task and questioned the amount of time George had estimated. The following conversation ensued in an open meeting:

LIN (PM): "Now about this task, you have estimated 40 hours to complete that?"

GEORGE (C): "Yes."

PM: "Don't you think that's a bit of overkill?"

C: "No, why?"

PM: "I know for a fact that it should only take 10 hours to do that task."

The last statement from Lin is the one that does not allow the escape strategy. In fact, it put George in a lose-lose situation. George has two choices:

Agree with the PM and allow the PM to think that George was overcharging.

Prove that it may actually take 40 hours, which will make the PM lose face in front of the team.

George had to stand behind his estimate, and ultimately the PM lost face in front of the project team. This scenario could have been avoided with an escape strategy. The escape strategy always allows a graceful exit. For instance, the PM Lin could have made the same point by saying any of the following:

"In my experience, it has taken 10 hours in the past. Why would this task take 40?"

"I may be missing a requirement. Does the 40 hours mean just this work?"

"Can you help me understand why this estimate seems to be longer than anticipated?"

The difference is that Lin can gracefully exit if he has truly misunderstood the requirement. Stating it as "I know for a fact," does not allow the graceful exit. Be sure that when stating a position in a meeting or launching a Patriot (or a Scud) that there is always an exit strategy.

Now that you understand the strategy of Patriots and Scuds, it's important to spend some time thinking about risk assessment for projects. It's also important to be able to protect yourself and your team from missiles and to know when to launch them, but it is difficult to adequately manage a project without understanding and being able to explain and manipulate risk.

A REAL RISK ASSESSMENT

Risk is one of the most discussed topics in project management. There are a great number of books, seminars, and products that promote how to identify, qualify, and quantify risks. Risk assessment is a tool to help a project manager (PM) identify potential risks on a project and help create an overall ranking of risk on the project. Most risk assessment tools end with an arbitrary number or a subjective ranking. For example, the end result of a risk assessment can be a score of 4.533 or "high." These types of scores probably mean as much to the PM filling out the risk assessment as they mean to you as you read this—next to nothing.

▓ Why Risk Is Important

PMs need data to support their contingency needs. Risk planning and management is a protection against cost and schedule expectations. In fact, Project Management Institute® teaches that a project plan can't be finalized unless risk planning is complete. A schedule can't be finalized unless risk has been accounted for. How can a PM leverage a subjective scoring model to obtain the necessary time and cost to account for risk? It is nearly impossible. In addition, many of the seminars, books, and products available do not help the PM account or plan for risk if nobody will show up to the risk meeting in the first place! This chapter provides the framework to lead a risk assessment and management evolution. It shows how to develop a process that will create a risk assessment that ends with a solid result such as, "There should be 10 to 15 days and $20,000 added to this plan based on factors that have occurred in the past."

■ The Risk Process

To create a shift in the risk management process, one must begin with the current risk process. The next few paragraphs offer a very brief overview of this concept. There are many resources available to learn more in depth about risk and risk management. This overview is intended to assist in the understanding of the risk assessment's evolution. Traditionally, most project management experts teach that the risk management process steps are:

- Risk identification
- Qualitative analysis
- Quantitative analysis
- Risk response planning
- Residual risk planning

The first step is to identify the potential risks. The team, either through a meeting or individually, identifies the potential items that could have an impact on the project's cost, schedule, or quality. The following documents are inputs into the risk-identification process:

- Scope statement
- Work breakdown structure
- Resource plan

- Network diagram
- Project schedule
- Budget
- Quality plan

Every document created and every plan made is an input to risk management. Risk is an important concept. It is designed to assist in managing the unknowns. The theory is that through proper risk management, allowances to cost and schedule will be made to ensure a successful project. Once a list of risks is identified, it is time to begin to perform qualitative risk analysis

Qualitative risk analysis is designed to sort and rank the identified risks so that the PM can prioritize the list appropriately. The team is supposed to go through each risk factor and identify the probability the risk will occur and if the risk occurs, what the impact will be on the project. In true project management practice, based on the qualitative analysis of risks, a project could be stopped if it is deemed too risky. Qualitative analysis is a subjective assessment of each risk and usually uses terms such as *high, medium,* and *low* to determine the overall ranking of the risk. High probability and high impact should be evaluated first, and low probability and low impact should be evaluated last. It is anyone's guess of how risky the item is to the project. At the end of qualitative analysis, a chart would look similar to Table 12-1.

Once the qualitative analysis is complete, quantitative analysis will begin to put values on the risk.

Quantitative analysis is a numerical analysis of each risk. For every risk, the team should decide the likelihood (represented as a percentage) that the risk will occur and the impact on the project's cost or timeline should it occur. This step removes the subjectivity of the qualitative

TABLE 12-1. QUALITATIVE RISK ASSESMENT

Risk	Category	Probability	Impact
Team members are unavailable for the project	Resources	Medium	High
Budget is not established	Budget	High	High
Technology has not been used before	Technology	Medium	Medium

analysis and focuses the PM on the risks with the highest impact. The highest dollar figure or highest impact on time should be planned for first. At the end of quantitative analysis, the chart would look like Table 12-2.

At the end of qualitative and quantitative analysis, the PM has a list of prioritized risks. The PM then needs to create a response plan to the risks. The general responses to a risk are:

Avoid: Eliminate the threat by eliminating the cause.

Mitigate: Reduce the probability or the impact of a threat.

Transfer: Make another party responsible.

Accept: If it happens, it happens.

Each risk should have a response plan. The plan is intended to either keep the risk from happening or limit the impact the risk will have on the overall project. For many people, this is a long and complicated process, however, it is not complete. The final step deals with residual risks.

Residual risks are risks that are created based on the strategy selected in the response-planning stage. For example, a risk for a construction project near the coastline is the potential of a hurricane. To transfer this risk, the construction company buys hurricane insurance to protect them from financial loss. The residual risk would be the potential for the insurance premiums to increase over time. The residual risk, the cost of premiums, was created by choosing the transfer strategy of the hurricane risk. Essentially, the team is supposed to now think of all of the things that could go wrong based on how the team chooses to deal with potential items that could go wrong. Confused? So are

TABLE 12-2.   RISK VALUES

Risk	Category	Probability	Impact	Total
Team members are unavailable for the project	Resources	60 percent	$10,000	$6,000
Budget is not established	Budget	80 percent	$50,000	$40,000
Technology has not been used before	Technology	35 percent	$5,000	$1,750

most PMs. What is worse, the PMs that understand this process have difficulty getting their team to understand the process.

▨ Why People Are Opposed to Risk Management

The process just explained is tedious and requires quite a bit of team-work. There is also a major flaw in the system. It is difficult to plan for risks when the team is not involved, and the team generally is not involved because they either do not understand why the process is valid or they do not see the value in completing the process. Sponsors are also considered to be a flaw in the system. One sponsor went on record as saying about a particular project, "This project has no risk because it has to be done on time." For the most part, people are opposed to risk management because they have never been a part of it or they have never directly attributed a project gain to it.

Anna was a new PM who had just finished a five-day course on risk management. She was so excited to apply the concepts and begin to account for risk on her project. She scheduled a team meeting and followed all of the proper meeting setup rules. She was immediately deflated when she showed up to the meeting, and less than 15 percent of the meeting invitees were present. She continued with the meeting but felt like she did not gain the value out of the meeting that she had hoped for due to such low turnout. When she began to question the absent team members, she heard several excuses:

"There is no risk in my area, so I didn't feel that I needed to be there."
"We have done this so many times; we already know how to deal with the potential risks."
"I didn't have time to sit around and dream about all of the things that might or might not happen on the project."

All excuses showed a lack of understanding of the risk process, however, what could Anna do? She could try to educate the team members or force meetings. But, risk identification is a creative process. If the team itself is not focused, then the proper creativity is not there. Unfortunately, many team members are apathetic to the risk management process. Many sponsors also do not understand how risk assessment can benefit them.

Another important reason people are opposed to the risk management process is that they see it as a negative process. Risk is about dealing with potential problems, and discussing them can be uncomfortable. There is a part of human nature that tends to avoid negativity, and discussing risk is seen as something that is negative. The truth is that risk assessment is a positive process because the team can collectively see the potential issues and create some solutions that anticipate issues and resolve them proactively. Unless the team has seen this work successfully already, however, they are usually reluctant to start a new process.

As we stated earlier, although there are many books, seminars, and workshops that discuss how to lead the meetings, perform risk management, and educate the team, there is a significant gap in these teachings, and it is one that new PMs discover. In the beginning of this chapter, we discussed the project office team that had to accelerate the discussed process and be accurate. Their challenge was to understand how they could account for risk when nobody will even show up to the meetings. How can the PM account for risk when nobody will even show up to the meetings? How can the PM plan for risk if the sponsor doesn't believe that there is any risk in the project? How can the PM be effective if the team is not supportive? The answer is through a dynamic risk assessment, and that is exactly what happened in our current example. It is not an easy process, and it is certainly not a quick fix. On the other hand, it is extremely effective and if done properly, it will begin to change the culture of risk and risk management in the organization.

▧ Dynamic Risk Assessment

The dynamic risk assessment is designed to assist PMs when their team does not support risk identification. It is not a quick fix or an immediate strategy and is instead an assessment that will evolve over time. In the beginning, it will be generic. With diligence and proper updating, the dynamic risk assessment will begin to provide immense value.

The beginning of the process is to establish a risk assessment, which is what the team in the current example did. It does not have to be fancy or elaborate; the important part is that the PM develops some discipline in filling out the assessment. One of the most quoted studies in project management is the CHAOS study published by the Standish

Group. In the study, they discussed the common areas that caused projects to fail. Here are some of the findings:

- Eighteen percent failed due to lack of executive support.
- Sixteen percent failed due to lack of user involvement.
- Fourteen percent failed because of an inexperienced PM.
- Twelve percent failed because the business objectives were unclear.
- Ten percent delivered a minimized scope but failed because the project did not deliver all of the requirements.

Many of the other factors include a lack of a formal methodology, poor estimates, and no standard software quality.

If projects consistently fail because of these factors listed, then the first places to truly identify relevant risks are in these categories. Using these categories as a guide, a PM can develop his or her own risk assessment questions or can find templates on the Web and categorize questions into the categories. The PM in our example did that. The initial step is to create an analysis that will assist in the identification and prioritization of risks. Some sample risk assessment questions are:

- Will this project change the workflow for a company, department, or person?
- Will this project have dedicated or shared resources?
- Are there multiple customers for the deliverables?
- Has a completion date for the project been set without the PM's involvement?
- Is there proper justification for executing the project?
- How involved will the executives be in the planning of the project?

These questions are tools to assist the PM in identifying the risk for a project as well as make the PM think of items that he or she may not have already considered.

The next step in creating the assessment is to quantify the answers to remove some of the subjectivity. For example, many assessments simply ask a PM to choose the likelihood of high, medium, or low risk as an answer to a question; however, these categories are quite subjective and can skew the results. What one manager may think is a high risk, another may think is a low risk. Therefore, for each question, the team quantified what makes an answer high, medium, or low. For example, the questions we just listed would appear as in Table 12-3.

One of the worst aspects about a risk assessment is the subjectivity. Qualifying what actually means *high, medium,* and *low* should keep the answers in sync regardless of the individual answering the questions. The team started with a generic risk assessment and began to utilize it on existing projects to get used to the process. Also, they tracked how the project actually performed and if any of the risks were realized.

TABLE 12-3.   *RISK ASSESSMENT QUESTIONS*

Item	High	Medium	Low
Will this project change the workflow for a company, department, or person?	Significant changes	Will change some aspect	No change to workflow
Will this project have dedicated or shared resources?	Shared resources across many projects	Some shared and some dedicated	Dedicated resources
Are there multiple customers for the deliverables?	Multiple customers with different wants/ needs	Multiple customers but have shared needs	Single customer
Has a completion date for the project been set without the PM's involvement?	Date set by executives with no outside involvement or is driven by market demands	Date set by team but is driven by market or regulatory demands	Date is being set by the planning process of the project
Is there proper justification for executing the project?	There is no satisfactory justification for the project	Some justification is provided	Justification is complete and accurate
How involved will the executives be in the planning of the project?	No support	Support through showing up to status meetings	Strong and visible support

▓ The Beginning of the Transformation

The first part of the risk assessment was designed to ensure that the team followed the process. After some time using the generic risk assessment, it was time to make the risk assessment more focused to the current company. For this portion to work, it is extremely important that the rules in Chapter 9 for a project plan are followed. If followed properly, then every project plan would have a baseline, and the actual results of each project would be consistently updated so that the planned values and the actual values would be present. The team used the past project plans as an input into the transformation of the risk assessment from a generic questionnaire to a culture-impacting activity. They examined each plan and found where tasks took longer than originally planned. Specifically, they looked for duration and cost variances that were above a certain threshold (such as a duration variance of 5 days or a cost overrun of $5,000). The logged the following information about each anomaly:

- Description
- The cause
- The project name
- The impact it had on the overall project

The team logged this information continuously. They started to create new categories based on the general findings. For instance, the categories can be related to specific departments such as finance, IT, or legal. The end result was a log of actual items that caused X issues to actual projects performed at the company. The log looked something like Table 12-4.

The potential categories for these risks could be legal, resources, and infrastructure, respectively. There are no right or wrong answers when it comes to the categorization, but it is important to have all questions in a category. The reason will be revealed later in the chapter. Also, it is important to track all variances over a certain threshold or defined level of impact such as anything causing a delay of more than 10 days, even if there is not an overall effect on the project. For example, the servers being late delayed a task but not the overall project. Applying the concepts learned throughout the book, if the task were late, but it did not have an impact on the end date of the project, what do we

TABLE 12-4.   TASK VARIANCE LOG

Variance	Cause	Project	Impact
15 days	Legal did not review contracts in time.	Project management system	Delayed the project completion date
$10,000/ 10 days	Key resource left the project midway through. Had to bring in a contractor to complete the job.	New Web site	Delayed the project completion date
15 days	Servers were delivered late.	Data Center Upgrade	No delay to the project; other items were in progress.

know about the task? The server delivery must not have been on the critical path. It may be a critical path item in a future project, however, so tracking the variance is extremely important.

After the team in our example identified several variances, the next step was to blend actual risk questions with the generic ones from the existing risk assessment. They also decided that this was a good time to begin to pull in other team members. They showed them the variances and asked them to proactively help in solving an issue before it occurs. It is the author's experience that the process becomes quite collaborative when real variances and real risks are identified. The team members begin to see the value of the exercise and will begin to assist.

There may still be cases in which the team will not participate or support the PM. It is always best to involve the team; however, there is enough information to progress to the next step of the risk system.

■ The Evolution of the Risk Assessment

The next stage of creating a real risk assessment deals with categorization, weighting, and the Program Evaluation Review Technique (PERT) formula. This is another area where it is best to have team involvement. (This system will, however, work with or without team involvement.) Using our current example, the team first established all of the categories (types) and weight of importance for the questions. These may or may not be the same categories that the original assessment carried. The team arrived at the following results as shown in Table 12-5.

TABLE 12-5.   *OLD VERSUS NEW ASSESSMENT CATEGORIES*

Original Assessment Categories	New Assessment Categories
Executive Support (18 percent)	Upper Management (12 percent)
IT (18 percent)	Scope/Business Case (10 percent)
User Involvement (15 percent)	Contract/Legal (16 percent)
Experienced PM (13 percent)	IT Department (14 percent)
Clear Business Objective (11 percent)	Vendor Risks (8 percent)
Team Experience (9 percent)	Resources (11 percent)
Standard Infrastructure (7 percent)	Technology/Product (8 percent)
Firm Basic Requirements (5 percent)	Schedule (9 percent)
Other Criteria (4 percent)	Project Management (5 percent)
	Other (7 percent)

The categories and the weights changed, but there is a definitive difference between the two lists. The first was composed of generic issues that *could* affect the organization. The second list comprises actual issues that *did* affect the organization. The second list contains the categories that were created from the list of variances the team discovered on projects.

The weights are also a very important factor. They will be used in a statistical formula in a moment; however, they are designed to be fluid. The goal of risk identification and assessments is to reduce the impact or probability that they will occur. The reason a weighting system is placed on the risk category is to separate more high-impact risks from lower-impact ones. In addition, it also allows the risk category to diminish over time. For example, a high-risk category in the second list was due to contracts and the legal process. The team had many issues getting contracts through the process. They also deemed this task the most likely to have a high impact on projects and gave it the highest category weight of 16 percent, which was the largest percentage in the second list. If the company were to focus and drastically improve the legal process within the company, then the risk percentage should decrease and potentially eliminate the risk category altogether. As the risks and the environment fluctuate, so should the category weights. To be effective, the category weights should always equal 100 percent.

The team also decided that each question would carry its own weight within the category. The weights should also equal 100 percent

TABLE 12-6.   TECHNOLOGY/PRODUCT QUESTIONS

Question	Weight
Are external customers affected?	10 percent
Will there be a pilot group for user testing?	25 percent
Has the team seen a demonstration of the product?	10 percent
Is this new technology for the organization?	20 percent
Is the organization the first to use the technology?	25 percent
Has the quality of the technology or the performance of the technology been identified?	10 percent

within each category. The rationale is the same. For example, in the second list of risk assessment categories, there is one named "Technology/Product." A breakdown of that category is shown in Table 12-6.

The question weights also equal 100 percent. What made this new approach so powerful was that each one of these questions was supported by an actual issue that caused a variance on a project within the organization. There were times when the team was unsure of which weight to assign. The answer depended on the impact the event had on the project. The larger the impact of the event, the larger the weight that should be assigned. It is easy to see that the team found larger impacts due to not having a pilot group to test new technology and that the organization was the first to use the technology or product. This is easily identified because these two areas had the largest amount of weight assigned.

To complete the risk assessment, the team identified two more areas to assign values, although they are pretty standard. The first set is to decide the numerical value of high, medium, and low responses. What they found worked best was to assign a value of one for low, two for medium, and three for high. The second set was to decide the best case and most likely values for the risks. The worst case was derived by the actual variance and extracted from the log that was created during the variance analysis phase. Best practice for the value of the best case of a risk is zero. The best case in a risk scenario is that the risk does not occur. The most likely value is generally set at 5 days. The team set this for statistical normalization, and most items of risk can be set in values of five. By this point, the following has occurred:

- Variances have been identified in past projects.
- A log has been created listing the variance and project.

- All variances were categorized into newly created categories.
- The categories were assigned weights equaling a total of 100 percent.
- Each variance created a question to ask on an assessment and has been assigned a weight totaling 100 percent within each category.
- Each question has an answer defining what constitutes a high, medium, or low response.
- The categories of high, medium, low, best case, and most likely all have standardized values that will be used throughout the assessment.

It was now time to bring all of the work together to produce the final product.

The Final Product

The end result for all of this work was for the team to be able to utilize historical data to develop a basis for adding time or cost to the project through contingency planning. The final product will use all of the categorization and variance tracking in conjunction with the PERT formulas discussed in Chapter 7. This would also allow the team to select an end date quicker by accelerating the risk process and have the reasons for selecting the amount of risk to add to the project. Each question was answered, and a value of high, medium, low, or not applicable is assigned for probability and impact. All of the information was then calculated through a formula to establish risk. The formula that should be used for this calculation is:

(Risk Best Case + (4* Risk Most Likely) + Risk Worst Case)/6) * Probability * Impact * Category Weight * Question Weight) = Risk Days

All of the values are then added up to equal the amount of risk that should be added into the project. Let's take the category above and show the results of the formulas. The PM in our example answered all of the questions and determined the probability (likelihood that the risk will occur) and the impact if the risk did occur to the project. From the PM's standpoint, all they are determining is those two values for each question on the assessment. All of the other calculations will occur behind the scenes. The Technology/Product section was answered with the values shown in Table 12-7.

The formula then calculates as shown in Table 12-8.

All of the values added together would equal 2.735333 (or rounded to 3) days of risk for the Technology/Product section of the risk assessment. Following this example all the way through, an end report would look like Table 12-9.

The final portion is to decide the range. This is generally done by the PM from experience, and that is how it worked in our example as well. There is also a mathematical way to calculate the range. The mathematical method involves calculating the standard deviation of the estimates (Worse Case – Best Case)/6) and creates the variance (Standard Deviation Squared). Whichever the case, the range will result in a number that will be added and subtracted from the number calculated to create the range of risk. In this example, the range was calculated to be 8 days. Therefore, the range of risk is between 22 and 38 days of risk and should be added to the project based on things that have occurred in the past.

We discuss how to put these numbers into a project plan in the next chapter. The team in our example found that the conversation of adding risk to the project changed with the sponsor or stakeholders of the project. Instead of stating that this project carries a score of 4.2434 or scored as a "high," which is the result of most risk assessments, the answer was now more direct. "Based on the projects in the past, variance analysis, and statistical formulas, this project is expected to be delayed by 30 days under the current circumstances." It is a much more

TABLE 12-7. COMPLETED QUESTIONNAIRE

Question	Probability	Impact
Are external customers affected?	Medium	Low
Will there be a pilot group for user testing?	High	High
Has the team seen a demonstration of the product?	Low	Low
Is this new technology for the organization?	Not applicable	Not applicable
Is the organization the first to use the technology?	High	High
Has the quality of the technology or the performance of the technology been identified?	Medium	Low

TABLE 12-8. QUESTIONNAIRE WITH FORMULAS

Question	Question Weight	Category Weight	Best Case	Most Likely	Worst Case	Proba-bility	Impact	Result
Are external customers affected?	10 percent	8 percent	0	5	12	2	1	0.085333
Will there be a pilot group for user testing?	25 percent	8 percent	0	5	15	3	3	1.05
Has the team seen a demonstration of the product?	10 percent	8 percent	0	5	5	1	1	0.033333
Is this new technology for the organization?	20 percent	8 percent	0	5	22	0	0	0
Is the organization the first to use the technology?	25 percent	8 percent	0	5	30	3	3	1.5
Has the quality of the technology or the performance of the technology been identified?	10 percent	8 percent	0	5	5	2	1	0.066667

TABLE 12-9.   TOTAL RISK DAYS

Category	Risk Days
Upper Management	3
Scope/Business Case	4
Contract/Legal	2
IT Department	5
Vendor Risks	5
Resources	2
Technology/Product	3
Schedule	4
Project Management	1
Other	1
Total	30

powerful conversation when there are facts, analysis, and formulas backing up the assessment.

The team created an application that performed all of the complex calculations, and in the end, created a printed report that they could attach to the project plan to show why the number of risk days was chosen. With the addition of this tool and utilizing the concepts discussed in earlier chapters, the team had a 98 percent success rate of completing a project on or before the end date selected.

▓ Involving the Team

Although there will still be times when the team will not be focused and will not support the risk assessment, it is the author's experience that when true results are seen and influential events are minimized due to proper risk management, the team will gladly participate. The first portion of the identification comes from variances found in past project plans. A great way to involve the team, other PMs, and a project management office (PMO) is to have an update strategy to the system. The system has several items that propel its value:

- It brings visibility to the highest probability and most high-impact risks in a repetitive fashion. If the source of the risk is not worked on, then each and every project will account for time and cost due to that risk. In essence, it gives a PMO a prioritized list of overall risks that should be eliminated, or it will affect all projects.

- It provides factual data about past variances and uses them to support a sound practice for contingency planning.
- It also assists in providing the right information (project name and actual variance) should there be a disagreement on the validity of the amount of contingency.
- It provides a direct correlation to past issues and current planning. This is a perfect example of how to use historical information to plan a project.

With all of these benefits, it is important to keep the assessment updated. If there is a PMO, hopefully he or she is reducing the risks with the highest impact. Therefore, the weights would need to be adjusted. There will be new variances as well as new projects, and the team's input would be invaluable to keep the assessment current. Why would the team support this system and not the meetings before? Simply put, the team can see the benefits of this system. Traditional risk systems hold meetings in which everyone sits around and thinks of things that can go wrong. This system uses examples of what actually did go wrong and assists in the prevention or mitigation of having them go wrong again.

Here is a generic process to keep the assessment updated:

- At the project's completion, team members and PMs submit a risk identification form to a central location (PMO if possible, and we will use the PMO as the example going forward). This form should include the cause, impact, and actual variance of a risk.
- The current risks in the system are evaluated and updated. New risks are added if necessary.
- The PMO continuously works on identified recurring risks and tries to lessen the impact on the organization.
- Categories, questions, and weights are reviewed and updated on a frequent basis.
- The PM completes the updated risk assessment when beginning a new project. He or she will determine the probability

and impact, and the risk assessment tool will establish the amount of risk. Risk is added to the project.

- The team and PM track any variances on the project.
- Repeat the cycle.

Team involvement is always best in any circumstance, but even if the team members do not support a risk assessment, a great tool can still be created to assist in the planning and assessment of risk in a project. It may appear to be a long and drawn-out system and a great deal of work, however, once set up, the system is fluid and will pay tremendous dividends down the road. In the next chapter, we discuss what to do with the risk now that it is identified.

HOW TO PUT RISK IN A PROJECT PLAN

I n the last chapter, we addressed how to accurately assess risk. The next step is inserting that risk into a project plan in a way that is usable and reliable. This chapter works through that process.

One of the most challenging tasks in project management is adding risk to your plan, without showing it to the team. In this chapter, we discuss some common rules for identifying and displaying risk, while also maintaining the risk as contingency. Risk and risk management largely become a trust issue. Most sponsors and stakeholders do not accept risk estimates because they view it as fluff or as having no real value to the project. In many cases, they are correct. If you utilize the concepts in this book, however, then risk is substantiated by data. The amount of risk to add to the project is based on the real risk assessment from Chapter 12 to determine real risk days and what has occurred in past projects, not fluff. Yet, it is not wise to publish the risk contingency for fear that the team will use it unnecessarily or that people will confuse a risk date with a real date. For example, if a project completion date is March 31 and the date with risk is April 17, the team might be confused and accept April 17 as the end date of the project. This chapter shows how to keep the planned risk internal to the project manager (PM) and prevent common risk-related issues from occurring.

▦ Thirteenth Floor Principle

The phrasing and order was chosen with care. Most PMs only have exposure to risk via the risk assessment, which is generally done in the initiation phase of the project. Risk management is done during planning, which follows the initiation phase. Risk assessments are normally the inputs to risk management. The discussion of the 13th floor principle will catch individuals who try to gloss over the assessment and will establish how to move risk to the forefront of the conversation.

We have saved the 13th floor principal for the 13th chapter of this book. To say that risk management in projects is misunderstood in an understatement. There is a key principle that proves the point: the 13th floor principle. This principle gets its name from the superstitious building developers and managers that skip naming a floor the 13th floor. On the elevator, the buttons will go from one to 12 and then skip to 14. This numbering system is set up is to lead us to believe that just because there is no 13th floor labeled, that one does not exist. In fact, the 14th floor is the 13th floor, just mislabeled. The same can be said about risk. Just because we do not show risk does not mean that risk does not exist. Earlier in this book, we talked about the sponsor who said, "There is no risk in this project because it has to be done on time." Project team members are conditioned to be afraid to acknowledge and plan for risk because of the lack of understanding that surrounds it. There are a few myths that have to be dispelled about risk.

MYTH 1: RISK IS BAD

Not all risk is negative. Risk can also have positive impacts on a project. For example, a company is completing a project to launch a new product into the marketplace. Each day, they launch before the competition, the more market share and more profit the company will make. An obvious risk would be to complete the project after the competition, but a positive outcome of the risk is that if the fear of finishing late causes the project team to find a way to complete the task even 2 weeks earlier, then risk management provided a positive outcome.

Myth 2: Risk Is Only Used to Pad Project Estimates

The first point to understand is that Project Management Institute® and the project management profession discourages and does not recognize padding. Padding means to arbitrarily add a number to an estimate. True PMs use statistical data and risk assessments like the one discussed in Chapter 12 to qualify and quantify the amount of risk added to a project.

Myth 3: Risk Management Is a Waste of Time

This is normally the decree of teams that have performed risk management but never felt the benefit of performing risk management. Unless the PM can quantify how risk management has saved the project team time or heartache, it is hard to prove this point. Therefore, the PM must constantly educate the team on how the exercises directly benefit them on their projects. In many cases, risk management keeps the team "out of the fire" when things go wrong because they were anticipated. Use this knowledge to show the value of risk management.

It is hard to dispel this myth, but it is worth the effort. A larger issue may be keeping the risk time quantified as risk time and not simply releasing it into the schedule. To understand this portion, we must first understand Parkinson's and Murphy's laws.

▨ Parkinson's Law

Parkinson's Law states "work expands to fill the time available." Relating this definition to the project world, if there is risk or any free time in the project plan, then the workers will fill it. To state it differently, if we were to ask you to complete a questionnaire and send it back to us by next Friday, when do you think it will be completed? Many people will answer next Friday. It is human nature to put things off until they are critically due. For example, people tend to procrastinate so much that the United States Post office has special hours and special procedures for April 15, the deadline for when taxes have to be postmarked and sent to the Internal Revenue Service. A need has been created because a date has been set. Although many individuals will complete their income tax filing sooner than April 15, there are enough people proving Parkinson's Law to warrant changes to a government agency's procedures.

It is also important to realize that most project team members work on multiple projects and generally have their own functional job as well. Therefore, if a task is going to take a day to complete but is not due for 2 weeks, then most likely, the task will be pushed off in favor of a task with a sooner due date. When applied to project management, Parkinson's Law means that if a PM shows the risk date, then team members will fill the time frame naturally to the later date. Therefore, PMs are often leery of publishing the risk date. Sponsors and stakeholders generally have past experience in seeing a project naturally fill a later date and do not want to allow a risk date. It is not always the project team's fault. Using the example stated earlier in this chapter, if the PM published a project plan that had April 17 (the risk date) as the completion date, people would just see that date and naturally push off their work. It is not done maliciously; the team members did not understand the difference between the two dates. Maybe they did not look at the plan closely enough or see that it was the date with risk. In any case, the time is usually utilized.

Inevitably, PMs become conditioned not to put risk into the project plan; however, another law is prevalent in project management. That law is Murphy's Law.

Murphy's Law

Murphy's Law means that anything that can go wrong, will and at the worst possible time. This law is proven time after time in projects. In fact, 2 percent of a project will always go wrong, but the question is, which 2 percent? Murphy's Law shows that risk must be accounted for. Something will go wrong on a project. It is the PM's job to anticipate what will go wrong and to perform proper risk planning to mitigate the impact on the project.

This situation creates a quandary for PMs. How can risk management be performed to account for Murphy's Law, yet not show risk to prevent Parkinson's Law? The answer isn't as complex as one may think. It is a technique that is used to set the proper context of the presentation of risk.

■ Putting Risk in a Project Plan

The first thing to do when placing risk in a project plan is to ensure that the plan has followed the rules established in this book. The tasks should be linked via predecessors and successors. Each task should have a duration, and if a task were to finish early or late, the plan would ebb and flow accordingly. This technique enables the PM to put risk into the plan, account for it, record the result, and then remove it. The benefits of the technique are as follows:

- Risk is a separate line item allowing a direct discussion with the sponsor about risk. It also eliminates the fear of adding fluff to the plan.
- When completed, the baseline will account for risk while the published schedule will show the most aggressive date.
- The risk is not published for the team preventing Parkinson's Law.
- The risk is still accounted for in the plan to assist with Murphy's Law.

To perform this technique, a PM should have access to a proper planning tool such as Microsoft Project or Open Workbench. For example, consider the following information, PM Cheryl has determined:

- Task 1 will take 5 business days to complete and can begin when the project begins.
- Task 2 must wait for Task 1 to finish and will take 2 business days to complete.
- Task 3 must wait for Task 2 to finish and will take 3 business days to complete.
- Task 4 must wait for Task 3 to finish and will take 10 business days to complete.
- A milestone will mark the completion of the four tasks and will be linked to Task 4 for the completion date.
- The team has used best-case, most-likely, and worst-case analysis to establish these estimates. Based on issues in the past, the team feels that there is a risk factor of 5 business days to complete the project.

TABLE 13-1. PLAN WITHOUT RISK

Task Name	Duration	Start	Finish	Predecessors
Task 1	5 business days	Mon. 9/3	Fri. 9/7	Start date
Task 2	2 business days	Mon. 9/10	Tue. 9/11	Task 1
Task 3	3 business days	Wed. 9/12	Fri. 9/14	Task 2
Task 4	10 business days	Mon. 9/17	Fri. 9/28	Task 3
Milestone	0 business days	Fri. 9/28	Fri. 9/28	Task 4

The plan, without risk, would look like Table 13-1.

Based on the plan without risk, the milestone would be completed on Friday 9/28. Now it is time to add the risk into the plan (Table 13-2).

The next step is to baseline the plan. A baseline is a line in the sand that will be used to compare the actual completion dates against the projected dates to determine if the project is ahead or behind schedule. When a plan is baselined, it copies the existing information for duration, start, and finish dates into a different column to preserve for comparison. Adding the baseline finish column to the view of the plan will produce results as shown in Table 13-3.

Once the plan is baselined, then the risk is accounted for in the measurements. It is time to remove the risk from the plan. When this occurs, the project plan will preserve the baseline finish dates but will reset the standard start and finish dates to their values without risk (Table 13-4).

The end result of the technique will show start and finish dates; however, the baseline finish of the milestone task will have a different date than the presented finish date, thus, accounting for Murphy's Law without allowing Parkinson's Law. To carry the technique further to a multiple

TABLE 13-2. PLAN WITH RISK

Task Name	Duration	Start	Finish	Predecessors
Task 1	5 business days	Mon. 9/3	Fri. 9/7	Start date
Task 2	2 business days	Mon. 9/10	Tue. 9/11	Task 1
Task 3	3 business days	Wed. 9/12	Fri. 9/14	Task 2
Task 4	10 business days	Mon. 9/17	Fri. 9/28	Task 3
Risk	5 business days	Mon. 10/1	Fri. 10/5	Task 4
Milestone	0 business days	Fri. 10/5	Fri. 10/5	Risk

TABLE 13-3.   *PLAN WITH RISK AND BASELINE*

Task Name	Duration	Start	Finish	Baseline Finish	Prede-cessors
Task 1	5 business days	Mon. 9/3	Fri. 9/7	Fri. 9/7	Start date
Task 2	2 business days	Mon. 9/10	Tue. 9/11	Tue. 9/11	Task 1
Task 3	3 business days	Wed. 9/12	Fri. 9/14	Fri. 9/14	Task 2
Task 4	10 business days	Mon. 9/17	Fri. 9/28	Fri. 9/28	Task 3
Risk	5 business days	Mon. 10/1	Fri. 10/5	Fri. 10/5	Task 4
Milestone	0 business days	Fri. 10/5	Fri. 10/5	Fri. 10/5	Risk

milestone plan, the next step is to link the first task of the second mile-stone to the first milestone. This stage will ensure that the start and finish dates of the next group of tasks will also account for risk. For example:

- Tasks 1 through 4 discussed previously are included in this plan. *Milestone* will be renamed to *Milestone 1*.
- Task 5 must wait for Milestone 1 to complete before it can begin and will take 3 business days.
- Task 6 must wait for Task 5 to complete and will take 2 business days.
- Milestone 2 will complete when Task 6 is complete.
- The team feels that there are 2 business days of risk in complet-ing Milestone 2.

The plan without risk would look like Table 13-5.

Adding the 5 business days of risk to Milestone 1 and 2 business days of risk to Milestone 2 and baselining the plan, the result would look like Table 13-6.

TABLE 13-4.   *PLAN WITH RISK DELETED AND BASELINE VISIBLE*

Task Name	Duration	Start	Finish	Baseline Finish	Prede-cessors
Task 1	5 business days	Mon. 9/3	Fri. 9/7	Fri. 9/7	Start date
Task 2	2 business days	Mon. 9/10	Tue. 9/11	Tue. 9/11	Task 1
Task 3	3 business days	Wed. 9/12	Fri. 9/14	Fri. 9/14	Task 2
Task 4	10 business days	Mon. 9/17	Fri. 9/28	Fri. 9/28	Task 3
Milestone	0 business days	Fri. 9/28	Fri. 9/28	Fri. 10/5	Task 4

TABLE 13-5.   *PLAN WITH LINKED MILESTONES*

Task Name	Duration	Start	Finish	Predecessors
Task 1	5 business days	Mon. 9/3	Fri. 9/7	Start date
Task 2	2 business days	Mon. 9/10	Tue. 9/11	Task 1
Task 3	3 business days	Wed. 9/12	Fri. 9/14	Task 2
Task 4	10 business days	Mon. 9/17	Fri. 9/28	Task 3
Milestone 1	0 business days	Fri. 9/28	Fri. 9/28	Task 4
Task 5	3 business days	Mon. 10/1	Wed. 10/3	Milestone 1
Task 6	2 business days	Thurs. 10/4	Fri. 10/5	Task 5
Milestone 2	0 business days	Fri. 10/5	Fri. 10/5	Task 6

Removing the risk would then produce the result as shown in Table 13-7.

TABLE 13-6.   *PLAN WITH RISK AND MILESTONES*

Task Name	Duration	Start	Finish	Baseline Finish	Prede-cessors
Task 1	5 business days	Mon. 9/3	Fri. 9/7	Fri. 9/7	Start date
Task 2	2 business days	Mon. 9/10	Tue. 9/11	Tue. 9/11	Task 1
Task 3	3 business days	Wed. 9/12	Fri. 9/14	Fri. 9/14	Task 2
Task 4	10 business days	Mon. 9/17	Fri. 9/28	Fri. 9/28	Task 3
Risk	5 business days	Mon. 10/1	Fri. 10/5	Fri. 10/5	Task 4
Milestone 1	0 business days	Fri. 10/5	Fri. 10/5	Fri. 10/5	Risk
Task 5	3 business days	Mon. 10/8	Wed. 10/10	Wed. 10/10	Milestone 1
Task 6	2 business days	Thurs. 10/11	Fri. 10/12	Fri. 10/12	Task 5
Risk	2 business days	Mon. 10/15	Tue. 10/16	Tue. 10/16	Task 6
Milestone 2	0 business days	Tue. 10/16	Tue. 10/16	Tue. 10/16	Risk

TABLE 13-7.   *PLAN WITH LINKED MILESTONES AND RISK REMOVED*

Task Name	Duration	Start	Finish	Baseline Finish	Prede-cessors
Task 1	5 business days	Mon. 9/3	Fri. 9/7	Fri. 9/7	Start date
Task 2	2 business days	Mon. 9/10	Tue. 9/11	Tue. 9/11	Task 1
Task 3	3 business days	Wed. 9/12	Fri. 9/14	Fri. 9/14	Task 2
Task 4	10 business days	Mon. 9/17	Fri. 9/28	Fri. 9/28	Task 3
Milestone 1	0 business days	Fri. 9/28	Fri. 9/28	Fri. 10/5	Risk
Task 5	3 business days	Mon. 10/1	Wed. 10/3	Wed. 10/10	Milestone 1
Task 6	2 business days	Thurs. 10/4	Fri. 10/5	Fri. 10/12	Task 5
Milestone 2	0 business days	Fri. 10/5	Fri. 10/5	Tue. 10/16	Risk

Based on the plan, if everything goes exactly as expected, the project is estimated to be complete by October 5. This is a planning technique. Later in the book, I discuss a real-world example of how to communicate this system. If the worst-case risks are realized, however, the project can be completed as late as October 16. Most PMs would like to publish the October 16 date to set proper expectations, but in the past, this has been detrimental because of Parkinson's Law. If October 16 is published as the completion date, then the likelihood of actually meeting the best-case date of October 5 is highly unlikely.

The other item to consider is that proper risk accounting is for the PM's benefit and necessarily for the team or the sponsor's benefit. The true reason for risk management is to establish the buffer zone of what should happen versus what could happen. The buffer zone is not for the team to use at their will or for the sponsor to remove. The buffer must be present to allow the PM to make adjustments and absorb issues while meeting the expected date. We discussed in great detail the context versus the content of the project in Chapter 4. This very quandary of PMs is the crux of that discussion. Through proper risk assessments, the team has identified risk. Placing the risk in the project plan shows a date of October 16. The best-case plan shows October 5, which is the plan that the PM wants to publish. The fear is, however, if that October 5 is the published date and if the project finishes on October 10, it appears that the project has failed, when in actuality, it completed early. The other fear is that if October 16 is published, that Parkinson's Law will take over. As the team is nearing the completion date of October 16, Murphy's Law occurs and causes the team to miss that date as well. By removing the risk from the project plan and not showing the baseline finish dates, the PM has successfully accounted for risk but has not shown it to the team. The final step in implementing this technique is selling the sponsor both dates.

▪ Presenting Risk to the Sponsor

The most important contextual date is the date the sponsor thinks that the project is committed to being complete. Utilizing the techniques in this chapter, there are two dates that have been established. October 5 is the best-case scenario date, while October 16 is the date that is the worst case if all planned risks occur. Selling this concept to the sponsor is actually a simple conversation that requires discussion and education about Parkinson's and Murphy's Laws. Once those are explained, the conversation goes something like this:

PM Kyle says to his sponsor, "The project will look to complete on October 16, however, I would like to show the most aggressive plan to the team at all times. The best-case scenario shows the project completing as early as October 5. I am going to publish the October 5 date to push the team to complete as quickly as they can, but the committed date with risk is October 16. Is this acceptable?"

Most sponsors will agree with this approach. Sponsors are generally against risk, not because they don't believe in the concept, but because they just feel that it is overused or added arbitrarily as fluff. Showing how the risk was accounted for, why it was added, and then removing it from the plan shows the sponsor that it is a planned event but not arbitrarily added. With the sponsor's approval, the plan can be published with a best-case scenario date in prevention of Parkinson's Law, while a communicated date between the PM and the sponsor accounts for Murphy's Law.

■ Presenting Risk to the Team

Some PMs feel that this technique is dishonest toward the project team. By not showing the risk, they may feel that the PM is discounting the project team's risk estimate. This is not the case. The PM must explain to the team that risk has been accounted for and that a discussion with the sponsor has occurred regarding the amount of and reasons for the risk. This explanation is followed by a discussion that if a risk occurs, the team will deal with it appropriately and adjust dates as necessary. The difference is that the end date with risk is not published, so the team is always focused on the best-case scenario date. If the PM has to move the end date, he or she can explain to the team that the end date has moved, but due to risk management, the sponsor does not see the project as late because of it. This will show the team that the risk hasn't been discounted and protects their perceptions of how risk is used.

Another way to avoid releasing a date to the team is to utilize to-do lists. Most project plans can be quite complex to read. Team members will rarely want to read a 300-page task project plan to find the two tasks that they are responsible for. Using to-do lists will publish a list of tasks to each team member with the proper start and finish dates without having to publish the entire project plan. There are tools in the marketplace that make this quite easy. For instance, a tool on www.moonlightit.com will take a Microsoft Project plan and create individually named Excel spreadsheets for each team member consisting of their to-do list. A tool like this would allow a PM to manage the complexity of a project plan with risk, while just showing each team member his or her piece of the overall plan.

In any case, the key is to not publish the plan with the risk dates exposed. Doing so would allow Parkinson's Law to take over and could eventually lead to project failure.

■ Using Risk

The final step to discuss is how to release the risk days to the team member if it becomes necessary. As previously discussed, risk contingencies are engineered for the PM's use. The risk is the PM's to manage. Proper project management will account for time and cost in a contingency bucket for the PM to use in situations when overruns are likely. If released too soon or if the contingencies are revealed and used without the PM's consent, then it is likely the project will fail. If a plan is published with risk dates and the team naturally fills the time frame allotted without the PM's consent, then an unexpected event that occurs will make the project late.

Through proper use, the PM can ensure that the team does not become overburdened, protect quality, and still meet an expected date. For instance, Task 1 on the project plan used earlier in this chapter is running late, so PM Jon contacted the team member (Tim) to receive a new estimate:

TEAM MEMBER TIM (TM): "I'm not going to finish Task 1 on time."

PROJECT MANAGER (PM): "When do you think you can have it done?"

TM: "If I work over the weekend, I can have it finished on Monday."

PM: "I appreciate the effort, but if you waited until Monday to complete the task, when do you think you could be done?"

TM: "Probably by Wednesday."

PM: "Is that your best-case estimate?"

TM: "Yes. Best case would be Wednesday."

PM: "Great. I'll plan on Wednesday, but if you need until Thursday, let me know. In fact, I will count on Thursday, but please do what you must to get it done by then. Is that fair?"

TM: "Fair. I will try to get it to you by Wednesday."

A couple of techniques were used in this scenario. First, Jon protected the team member from working all weekend, which is not always necessary. There may be a time when that is necessary, but it should not be the first choice. Jon also qualified the estimate the team member produced by asking the best-case question. In the end, Jon chose to use 4 days of risk to complete the task. There were 5 days of risk available to him. This still allows for another task to complete late while protecting the end date of the project. Of course, there are many examples to consider, but this is a quick illustration of how to use the technique.

In review, how to place risk in a plan to account for Murphy's Law while avoiding Parkinson's Law is as follows:

- Get proper risk estimates from the team.
- Set up the project plan properly.

- Put risk into each milestone or group in the plan.
- Baseline the plan.
- Remove the risk.
- Agree to the worst-case date with the sponsor.
- Publish the plan with the best-case date. Use to-do lists if possible.
- Use the risk days as necessary to bring the project plan back on track.

This process has been used many times with great success. It is effective in allowing the PM to manage the risk days and control the context of the project.

DATA RULES ALL!

W e've just spent some time talking about risk, which is calculation that relies on data. Many project managers (PMs) understand how to calculate risk and use the Program Evaluation Review Technique (PERT), yet when it comes time to talk to a sponsor about a project, they forget all the data they have accumulated throughout the project and its planning.

Experience in project management will tell you that it is hard to argue with data. Good data can ease the burden of any tough conversation. Throughout this book, we have discussed how to obtain and collect great information. It's now time to learn how to use the information you have gathered for the betterment of the project. Unfortunately, many very experienced PMs have not learned that data must be at the core of all discussions and decisions. In this chapter, we explain how to bring data into every aspect of project planning and management.

▣ Collecting Data

The project plan is the source for most of the data necessary to run a project. As discussed earlier in this book, making sure that the plan can ebb and flow as tasks finish early or late is one of the key focus areas for PMs. We have also discussed baselining a plan to ensure that it can be measured against. Doing so will allow the collection of variance data. Chapter 12 showed how to utilize the variance data as it pertains to risk, however, there are many other variances to consider. A PM has up to four different baselines to a project plan. They are:

Baseline 1: What the PM thought would happen prior to team input. This baseline is used to judge how well the PM understood the project at the beginning. The PM can ascertain how well he or she did or didn't understand the project at its inception.

Baseline 2: The original estimates from the team. Project planning is an iterative process. This baseline stores what the team had originally estimated to complete the project.

Baseline 3: The result of the plan after the sponsor provided input. Most sponsors will make adjustments based on the original estimates. For instance, if the planned date was after the desired date, the sponsor may make cuts or try to accelerate the schedule. Some sponsors will arbitrarily cut estimates. Whatever the case may be, this baseline tracks the end result of the sponsor involvement.

Baseline 4: The actual agreed upon date. This baseline is the baseline used for tracking.

Most PMs are unaware that multiple baselines can be saved inside a project plan. Tools such as Microsoft Project and Open Workbench allow this. PMs are sometimes afraid to baseline the plan at all or wait to baseline until it is as close to perfect as they can make it. Baselining the plan does nothing but copy over the existing information about a task into other columns for comparison later. If a task did not exist prior to the baselining of a plan, then the baseline finish for the plan will register as "not applicable." This will not affect any of the overall variance data. Therefore, it is best to create multiple baselines. The PM that uses this multiple baseline technique can derive the following information:

Baseline 1 Versus Actuals: This comparison will show how well the PM understood the project. This helps track how well he or she can estimate the project based on limited information.

Baseline 2 Versus Actuals: This comparison will show how accurately the team estimated the project.

Baseline 3 Versus Actuals: This comparison will track the result of the sponsor's involvement. For instance, if the sponsor arbitrarily cut the estimates, how well did the team do against the new estimates?

Baseline 4 Versus Actuals: This is the baseline comparison that is utilized to judge the overall project performance.

Some people question why it is important to track multiple baselines. The answer is to collect as much variance information as possible. Through diligence and proper plan updates, the multiple baseline technique can show patterns that may not be apparent. For example:

- How well did the team do against what they thought? (Baseline 2 variances)
- How did each individual team member do against his or her estimates? If there are variances, what was the percentage of difference? (Baseline 2 variances)
- How well did the PM understand the project before team involvement? (Baseline 1 variances)
- What was the result of what the team estimated versus what the sponsor allowed to be estimated? (Comparison of Baseline 2 and Baseline 3 variances)
- Did the project meet objectives? (Baseline 4 variances)
- If the project did not meet objectives, did they if Baseline 2 or Baseline 3 were effective?

Pulling this information from many different project plans will begin to show patterns. It may become apparent that one resource consistently misses his or her estimates by 25 percent, or that a certain sponsor always cuts 10 percent of the plan, or that the plans met the team estimates but not the expectations of the sponsor. Whatever the case may be, the data becomes priceless.

Consider this example. David was a PM who just finished putting together a project plan for a client that included estimates for a scope of work. The client questioned the number of hours that it took to do the work. The client's expectation was that the work should be a bit more inexpensive than estimated. This is a common discussion for many vendors and clients. David responded by showing each resource's best-case, most-likely, and worst-case estimates. He then showed the client that over the last five projects, the first resource was usually about 10 + percent above his best-case estimates, while the other resource was usually about 35 percent above his most-likely estimates. Utilizing the past history and applying the PERT formulas, David showed the client the math on how he developed the estimate. The client was blown away. Not only had David handled the client's objections, he gave a renewed confidence to the client that they were the vendor of choice. Most vendors had never discussed with this client how they actually create an estimate, thus always causing a bit of mistrust, but this PM showed with confidence that the vendor's team was honest, reliable, and knew their business. He was able to do this through due diligence work and the proper use of project data.

Using multiple baselines and keeping up with actual work completed is the most effective way to capture and collect the relevant data. There are many other sources that can be mined for this type of data as well. One of those sources is meeting notes. Meeting notes are usually used as historical records of meetings to document key decisions, track progress, and communicate status. There are also are many trends in meetings. One trend is to utilize a repository to store meeting notes. Whether this is done using a simple Access database or a more sophisticated solution such as a document management system, storing the notes so they can be accessed later is very important.

When considering meeting notes, it is vital to look beyond the normal details of a meeting and pick up trends. Some trends that can be found in meeting notes are:

- Average attendance of a team member throughout the project. Are the key people missing at key times? Does attendance start strong and then falter toward the end? When there is a key issue, does a resource decide to miss that meeting?
- Who is present when key decisions are made? Has there been a time on a project when a key decision was made when the spon-

sor was not present? A simple tracking of when a meeting was extremely productive or pivotal and who was present can shed some light on who the key players of the project are.

- Issue completion statistics and meeting preparedness. Who comes prepared to the meeting and who does not? Who consistently closed their action items from meetings and who always pushed them to the next week?

These appear to be minor items, but they are key to finding project success. Most projects do not fail in straightforward way. There are subtle trends and items that can forecast a project failing, and if you can pick these out, you will be able to better control the project and better predict completion in the future. For instance, if a certain resource is absent, and key items are not resolved, this is important in the short term to the individual project. On the other hand, if a trend develops with this resource, then a bigger problem may be in sight, which needs to be extrapolated onto future projects.

There are often patterns that can be found in project failure. Consider this example. PM Leila was running an IT support project. She kept track of what the quality items were that would cause a team to miss their service-level agreement. If the service-level agreement were to install a new PC 10 days after notification, if the company took longer, Leila would track the variance and the cause. She knew that the important part is to find the pattern. Sometimes, there would be many misses due to the cables not being run appropriately, and in these instances, Leila could address the cabling company and to resolve the problem. Sometimes, it was network IDs, bad hardware, missing information, and so forth. In one case, there seemed to be many misses regarding a certain department, although there was no apparent pattern. It seemed to be random misses. Out of 10 opportunities, two were missed due to cabling, two were missed due to network IDs, three were missed due to missing information, and the other four were random events. By considering the misses, Leila was able to look at the information several ways. She could see the technician on the calls, but there were five different technicians. She could see the buildings and locations, but these were also different. Finally, she found the pattern. The same person initiated all 10 items. He was new and did not know the normal process of requesting new PCs. Leila trained the new person, and the issues were alleviated.

Sometimes, the pattern is not apparent. PMs tend to address the actual issue instead of searching for patterns that link the issues. Searching for, collecting data, and creating unique ways of looking at the data will find patterns. These patterns exist in project plans and any project documentation. Locating patterns takes diligence, but the payoff is enormous.

■ Mining Data from Lessons Learned

We've talked earlier about how to complete "lessons learned." It is important that as a PM that you go beyond simply compiling lessons learned and develop the skill to use the data it contains. "Lessons learned" is one of the most underutilized project management techniques and also one of the most misunderstood. To many, lessons learned is simply a check box at the end of a project on the project list of items to do. The team members are told that they must come together and develop a list of lessons learned. The problem is, what happens to the list *after* it is created?

The reason lessons learned rarely provides results is because the lessons-learned document is never stored in a place where it can be used or reused properly. Lessons-learned results normally are found either on the PM's computer or in a network drive in a folder related to the project. This means that if there are 50 projects, there are 50 different lessons-learned documents residing in 50 different locations. And if a PM leaves, the lessons learned are essentially lessons forgotten because they cannot be found or used. The point of a lessons-learned document is to bring the lesson forward so that project's issues or mistakes can be avoided the next time. How is this possible if the documents are spread out everywhere and are unmanaged? Also, how does anyone determine what lessons are in what document? It is against human nature to navigate to 50 different documents, print them, read them, and try to ascertain how they will affect the project. The way to make these documents usable is to create a repository.

A proper repository will allow efficient use of the data. You can use a tool found on www.PM4u.net to create a database reference of lessons learned. At the end of the project, the PM enters the lessons learned about the project into the repository. At the beginning of the next project, that PM enters the known team members, technology, sponsors, and vendors, and a customized list of lessons learned is returned. This list provides the lessons that have been learned on past projects dealing with the same people, technology, or process. The important and relevant lessons learned are presented to the PM. Doing so allows the results to be readily available for use by all PMs in the organization in an efficient manner.

■ Making Emotional Conversations Unemotional

The end result of all the data collection and variance analysis this book has led you through is to come to an understanding of the real data, so that you can use it in real life to improve your projects. The real data is what it is. There is no magic or man behind a curtain. Data will rule all of the conversations you have about a project. Having good data can turn an emotional complaint from a team member into an unemotional fact-based conversation. Several conversations that normally have emotional connotations can, with the proper data, become unemotional discussions. Generally, these discussions revolve around mandated dates, issue resolution, and the overutilization of the team.

A mandated date is normally the first source of emotional conversations. PMs and team members can often be heard saying things like, "That can't possibly be done by that date," or "That date is impossible!" These comments are normally made to each other and not in front of the sponsor. If they are taken to the sponsor, they are usually greeted with disdain, giving the impression that the sponsor is unreasonable. The fact is that the person presenting the argument is not giving the sponsor a solution, they are complaining about an issue. The truth is that most mandated dates, as we've already discussed, are not really mandated. They are a convenient date or a date picked out of the air. The problem is that unless challenged, those dates become real. When the PM presents the argument that it simply can't be done, there are rarely any true facts supporting his or her position. Without the facts, the PM sounds like Charlie Brown's teacher, "Whaa wuh whaa wuh." Essentially, the emotional conversation tells the sponsor that the PM lacks the leadership skills to bring the project in on time. Using the facts can change the conversation. In Chapter 9, we discussed the rules for a project plan and the different cases of what to do with the actual date versus the desired date. Having the proper information will lead to a much more fact-based and unemotional conversation with the sponsor.

For example, Antoine was the PM putting in a project management system for a client. When Antoine received the project from his company, he was told that the project must be complete by March 31. When he arrived on site, he heard the same message from all of the project team members—how unfair the date was and how unlikely it was that the team could meet March 31. One team member remarked, "That's what the sponsor wants, so we will just have to figure out a way to do it." Already, the team was looking at what requirements they could remove from the project and how to downgrade the deliverables to fit into the mandated date. All of this occurred before Antoine could even start the planning process. When he went to start the project plan, the team was resistant because of the mandated date. Comments were made such as, "We don't have time to plan; we have to go forward to meet this date." Antoine still insisted on getting the team together and planning the project. He asked the team if anyone had had a conversation with the sponsor to understand why the date of March 31 was so important. The team had not. He instructed the team to plan the project without dates. Antoine asked for tasks, durations, and predecessors. He did not want to hear any dates. When he collected all of the tasks, the date fell on April 12. The team was again whipped into a frenzy of what to do. More meetings were held to discuss how the date could not be met, yet nobody had discussed this with the sponsor. Antoine wanted to hold a kick-off meeting and have a conversation with the entire team about the project end date.

At the meeting, Antoine opened with the general information about the project. About 10 minutes into the meeting, he showed the planned date of April 12. The conversation with the sponsor went like this:

ANTOINE (PM): "I know that you've requested the date of March 31 for this product to go live, but right now, the plan is showing April 12. The team and I will do everything we can to hit the March 31 date. Can I ask, what is the importance of March 31?"

SPONSOR (SPN): "No importance. March 31 sounded good because it was the end of the quarter. April 12 is fine."

PM: "All right, but as a team, we will do as much as we can to hit the March 31 date."

SPN: "Fair enough."

The team was dumbfounded. They had easily wasted 3 to 4 hours each of their time dealing with what they thought was a mandated date. In the end, the sponsor came back to Antoine and stated that he wanted a full quarter's worth of data in the system, so if the project went past March 31, they needed to find a way to ensure the data would be collected for entry. Antoine then had his contingency to missing March 31. Once the burden of hitting what the team felt was an impossible date was removed, they actually finished on March 24. The key to the conversation was the facts of the plan. Antoine did not disagree with the date; he simply showed the plan and discussed what the team felt they could do. Then he asked how important the mandated date was. If the sponsor came back with a stern March 31, then the team would have to deal with that, but at least the date would then be qualified.

Having the facts on your side will reveal the truth without political ramifications. Major mistakes are made when emotions become involved. Another example involves Carmen, a PM who was leading a funds transfer between holding organizations. This is an extremely regulatory process that requires many checks and balances. Once the funds were moved between the organizations, an oversight was found. A regulatory fine was being handed out to the company. The company's trustee was on a witch-hunt. A team meeting was called, and the trustee blamed Carmen for the mistakes. There were many instances that Carmen could recall in which the trustee had been notified of or even approved the move of the funds. In any case, because Carmen did not have the facts readily available, she chose to wait until the end of the meeting, gather the appropriate facts, and then discuss them. The trustee continued to rant and rave and called for Carmen's job due to the failure. After the team meeting concluded, Carmen went to her meeting notes repository and typed in the key words that she was looking for. She was presented with times, dates, and documentation of the conversations that she had recalled. Later that day, she was called into her boss's office where the trustee was present. It was clear that the trustee was going to allow Carmen to take the fall for the regulatory fine. In a clear and unemotional way, Carmen relayed the facts of the meetings, notes, and results, as well as the distribution of the notes. What had really occurred was that the trustee was the one who authorized the movement of the funds, not Carmen. The end result was the trustee losing his position. Unfortunately, this is a common occurrence. A PM who is completely responsible for the project tends to wind up in situations that could cost her the position. In times of great opportunity come either great rewards or great peril. Had Carmen lost her temper in the meeting and become emotional as well, then relationships could have become strained. Additionally, Carmen could have also stated errant information in the heat of the moment. The proper reaction is that of calm reserve and fact sharing. Had Carmen challenged the trustee openly and failed, then the end result would have been the loss of her job. Understanding that the unemotional telling of factual data will normally win disagreements, Carmen made the right move.

■ "Drop Everything" Does Not Mean Drop Everything!

A common mistake that PMs can make is to actually believe a sponsor when she says, "Drop everything and get this project done!" This is often a figure of speech that is used and one that many PMs will take literally. In reality, *drop everything* means to focus on this new priority, while trying to juggle the other priorities. For example, here is a conversation between a sponsor and PM Tyler:

SPONSOR (SPN): "I need you to drop everything and push this change through to production."

TYLER (PM): "Okay."

(Three weeks later)

SPN: "Why are we so behind on this project? This is a strategic project that absolutely needs to be done on time!"

PM: "You asked me to drop everything to get the other change completed. We did not work on this project while we completed that change."

SPN: "I didn't know that the change would have an impact on that project. I would have never let that happen. I need you to drop everything else and get this project in on time."

Of course, Tyler is scratching his head, wondering how the sponsor could be unaware that dropping everything would affect the strategic project. The answer is that he assumed that the sponsor really meant to drop everything. This was not the intent. Instead, the PM should have quantified the impact of the request. For example:

SPN: "I need you to drop everything and push this change through to production."

PM: "I understand. To complete this change, I will need to delay the strategic project by 3 weeks."

SPN: "We can't delay that project."

PM: "The resources needed to complete this change are on the strategic project."

SPN: "I need both completed."

PM: "Let's look at some options of how we can try to accomplish both."

In this case, Tyler did not assume that the sponsor wanted to truly drop everything. He quantified what the impact of the request would be to the sponsor. In the end, they came to an agreement of how to complete both in an acceptable time frame.

▒ Using Data in Conflict Situations

We have previously discussed the "it is what it is" attitude. This mindset becomes crucial when using data in conflict situations. The most common conflict stems from the negotiation for more time or a greater budget with a project sponsor. This is a common source of conflict because the dates and budgets are usually selected without proper project planning, leading to unrealistic time frames and expectations. Utilizing data can assist in these sometimes-tense situations. Usually, a PM will state that the project can't be completed in the time frame or for the cost selected. The sponsor then asks why. An unprepared PM will have an answer such as the team is too busy or the costs will be greater but does not have facts to back it up. Using the method provided in this book, the conversation should go more like this:

PROJECT MANAGER EVA (PM): "I need your help with the project commitments."

SPONSOR (SPN): "Sure, what is it?"

PM: "I've been given the date of March 31 and a budget of $50,000 to complete this project. According to the plan, with the resources allocated, I can meet the budget of $50,000. The date, however, is coming in at April 15. Either we can leave the date at April 15, or we can accelerate the schedule. Accelerating the schedule will cost an additional $5,000."

SPN: "Why will it cost more? I want March 31, but I have no more budget to spend."

PM: "Let me show you the plan. If we remove this requirement, then we can meet the March 31 date without accelerating the schedule or cost, but we will not have that requirement. What would you like to do?"

SPN: "Not much I can do. Can we do this other requirement at a later time?"

PM: "Under a new scope, sure. Would you like me to remove the requirement?"

SPN: "Will that get me to March 31 for $50,000?"

PM: "Yes."

SPN: "Then do it."

PM: "I'll draw up a change request for your signature."

Notice how the conversation remained factual? This kind of conversation can get quickly out of hand, but there was a subtle technique used in the delivery. That technique is to not say "no" but rather, "That absolutely can be done, here are the impacts." So many PMs feel that they have to become gatekeepers and for the most part, that is true. They also become emotionally involved to the point that they begin to take sides. When a PM begins to care which side of the argument wins, he or she is becoming too involved. In the end, the PM is there to plan and present options to the sponsor. The sponsor should be the one to make the decision about which way to proceed on the project, although many PMs do not take this step. Instead, they think that they understand what the sponsor wants and make decisions on the sponsor's behalf. They may try to get the project done by a certain time, and if they can't, they begin removing quality or requirements in order to make the date. They do this because they are afraid to have the tough conversations with the client or sponsor. It is acceptable to present options and request a decision from the sponsor as long as there are facts to back up the request. The important part is to remain neutral about the outcome of the situation. Simply present fact-based options and address the issue.

For example, Emil was the PM running a development project that was 3 months past due. The client and Emil were working together to wrap up the project as quickly as possible. The lead developer talked to Emil and said that the travel to the client location had worn him down. He would appreciate the ability to work remotely for at least 2 weeks to recharge. He also felt that the time would allow him to finish more quickly and work with fewer interruptions. The developer also said that if his wish was not granted, he was so burned out that he would probably leave the project. Emil went to the client sponsor to gain acceptance of the request. The following conversation ensued:

Emil (PM): "The lead developer is feeling burned out and has requested the ability to work remotely over the next 2 weeks."

Client Sponsor (CS): "Absolutely not! We need to finish this project, and we are already too far behind."

PM: "I understand and recognize the importance of the project. He really feels he is burned out on the project and needs the time at home to recharge. He has assured me that he would be more productive if we granted the request."

CS: "Do you think he would be more productive?"

PM: "Only time can tell. He has been true to his word so far. He has also been working long hours here, so I don't think it is a question of motivation. If we go against the request, it is likely he may leave the project."

CS: "I want him here. I need to see him here in order to trust that the work is getting completed."

PM: "I understand. Here are our options: I can force him to return next week, which will likely be a deterrent and may lead to him leaving the project, or we can grant his wish and trust him to complete his work. Whichever your decision, I will support it. It will likely take me 2 weeks to replace the development lead and bring someone else up to speed. It could be the same 2 weeks lost if he takes the time and does not complete his work."

CS: "Are you saying that we should grant the request and begin to look for a new team lead?"

PM: "I'm just presenting options. If we grant the request, and he does everything he promises, the project is in good shape. If he does not do what he promises, I will have already started on identifying a new team lead. The worst impact would be roughly 2 weeks."

CS: "Do that. He can work off-site, but I want him gone if we don't see the productivity."

PM: "Will do."

The end result of this decision granted the development lead the requested time. He took 2 weeks at his home office and worked remotely. He also completed an estimated 4 weeks worth of work within the 2 weeks. He was so productive that he never returned to the client site and completed the rest of the project remotely. Early in the conversation, the client was steadfastly against the remote idea. Emil really wanted to grant the time to the development lead. If Emil had become emotional as soon as the client had said no to the idea, then most likely, the request would have never been granted. By staying neutral and presenting options, the client came to the decision that the PM felt was best.

Becoming emotional and not relying on the facts can become a detriment to the project and the relationship with the sponsor or customer. If Emil did become emotional in the conversation relayed previously, the outcome could have been a tear in the relationship so great that it might not have been able to be repaired. Emotional conversations without facts tend to deal with feelings and general statements versus directed facts. Let's look at the very same conversation, this time with a more emotional and non–fact-based approach:

EMIL (PM): "The lead developer is feeling burned out and has requested the ability to work remotely over the next 2 weeks."

CLIENT SPONSOR (CS): "Absolutely not! We need to finish this project, and we are already too far behind."

PM: "Pushing our guys too hard will not work either."

CS: "Do you think he would be more productive?"

PM: "I just know he needs time off."

CS: "I want him here. I need to see him here in order to trust that the work is getting completed."

PM: "Are you saying that he can't complete his work off-site? You don't trust us?"

CS: "We are behind schedule, and now you want your team to take a break? We have clients and deadlines here, too. Although we work harder to meet our clients' needs."

PM: "We are working hard to meet your needs."

CS: "Who is asking for some time to recharge?"

PM: "Fine. I will tell him he can't. If he quits, we will have to deal with it."

The emotional conversation can lead quickly down a path that is not effective for the PM or the client. As the conversation becomes emotional, more general statements are made. Most likely, the general statements are little jabs at the other person, which can lead to hurt feelings or a strained relationship. If, however, the conversation remains fact-based and unemotional, the chances are greater that an amicable solution can be reached.

A PM's role is to deliver on the expectations of the project. Many PMs become upset or frustrated on a project that has many changes or phases. Dealing with these changes in direction is part of the PM's responsibility. Throughout this book, we have talked about how a PM should assess a change or request and notify the sponsor of the impact on the project. To be effective, this conversation must be done in a fact-based manner. PM Gemma shared a story of a discussion that never seemed to end:

GEMMA (PM): "To complete this project by the date requested, we either need to remove a requirement or add $25,000 to the budget for another resource."

SPONSOR (SPN): "I don't have $25,000 to spend."

PM: "Which requirement should we remove?"

SPN: "I want everything in there."

PM: "All right, is it acceptable to move the desired date?"

SPN: "No, I need it by that date."

PM: "In order to deliver by that date, I need to either remove a requirement or increase the budget. Which would you prefer?"

SPN: "I already said no to both."

PM: "So you would like me to deliver on this date without removing scope or increasing the budget?"

SPN: "Yes."

PM: "Do you not trust the team or these estimates?"

SPN: "I trust the team."

PM: "The team is saying that they need more time or resources."

SPN: "I need that date."

PM: "According to the plan, we are not saying it is impossible, but it is very unlikely to deliver this scope in the time frame allotted. It is likely that this project will fail before it begins."

SPN: "Are you saying that you can't run the project?"

PM: "Not at all. We will do our best to deliver this scope in the time frame allotted. We have asked for the time and resources necessary and have been declined. We will work with what we have to try our best to deliver."

SPN: "Great."

Of course, the project did go past the due date, and the sponsor continuously declined to reduce scope, however, he did not blame Gemma. This is not a case of winning or losing, and that is not what is important. It is important to stick to the facts and stay neutral to the conversation. The PM must present options. In the end, the sponsor will have to deal with the consequences of the decisions made.

The real point of all of this is that staying unemotional and sticking to fact-based arguments will benefit the PM. All issues can eventually be resolved by data. Find the data and the variances, and the issues will be solved. This is the same theory that process improvement strategies, such as Six Sigma, are built on. Six Sigma was created in the manufacturing world. It literally means "three defects per million opportunities." The entire course centers on identifying the process, finding the measurement points, and gathering data. Then, when a process enhancement is implemented, the data is measured again and compared against the original to validate the improvement. The same concepts are displayed in project management. Every decision in a project will have an impact on time, cost, resources, or quality. Find the data, present the options, and then deal with the change. Whether a sponsor grants more time or not, having the "it is what it is" attitude will allow the conversation to remain factual and unemotional. Presenting the data in an honest way will assist in coming to the best decision possible for the project and in turn, improve the chances for project success.

■ Countering Data That Is Harmful to the Project

There is no magic formula to counter data that is harmful to the project. The data is what it is and should be presented as such. If you utilize the concepts in this book, however, remember that harmful data should be found earlier in the project and dealt with in a timely manner. The decision to degrade quality, remove scope, or increase cost is that of the sponsor, not the PM. Therefore, the sooner that a variance is noted and presented, the more options the sponsor has to rectify the issue. The later the data is found, the fewer the options.

Another way to approach harmful data is to make sure that it is quantified. For instance, a company outsourced their computer repair operations to a vendor. The vendor was consistently berated over lack of performance or chastised for being late on a request. The issue was that there was no definition of what the performance standards were. In Chapter 8, it was stated that performance of an application should be a requirement. The same is true for measuring the performance of a task. The vendor became frustrated because only 2 percent of the completed tasks had issues. Unfortunately, the only items that were being discussed were the same 2 percent. The vendor quickly needed to find a way to establish the other 98 percent and took the following steps:

- Define what constitutes late or on time from a performance standpoint. Determine what the service level agreement is that they were agreeing to.
- Measure all activities against those standards. This provided visibility into the 98 percent that was going as planned and diminished the impact of the 2 percent that was consistently being discussed.
- Institute a customer satisfaction survey. The survey is left after each transaction so that each and every customer has an opportunity to complain or give praise.
- Ensure that the surveys are being consistently left by asking each person who complains or has an issue whether or not he or she

received a survey. If the answer is no, then one was immediately sent over, and the technician on that particular job was notified.

- Each negative comment received was handled with a phone call from the PM to validate and respond to the complaint.
- All metrics were tracked and reported.

Very quickly, the vendor was able to show over a 99 percent satisfaction rating and was able to proactively deal with issues. This data was used not only to counter harmful data but also to provide the appropriate perspective. Most of the time, executives only hear about the 2 percent of the project that will go wrong. It is the PM's responsibility to ensure that the other 98 percent is represented.

PROJECT MANAGER: THE STRATEGIC RESOURCE

You're aware of how the project management profession has simply exploded in recent years, as this role in a company or on a team continues to become more important. The most exciting trend, however, is how project management is becoming a strategic resource. In the early days of project management, it was dominated by charts, graphs, boring meetings, and statistical reporting. To be successful as a strategic resource, project managers (PMs) must now be change agents, influencers, and motivators, in addition to understanding trends and graphs. Today's PM needs to be able to influence and sell a team on why they want to complete projects on time or why a sponsor needs to invest more money into a project. PMs must manage all the personalities in a team and be able to influence sponsors and C-level executives. The days of simply reporting results are over. PMs are now proactive and forward-thinking enablers for the organization. They must be a strategic resource to be successful. This chapter discusses how to take on this role and how to effectively use strategy to get your job done.

▦ Needing the Data

The change in the role of PM from a passive resource to a strategic resource has been brought about over the last few years. Technology has assisted in this transformation, but the underlying cause has been the need for data. There have been several main drivers for this change:

- **The Year 2000 project:** Many companies overspent and overstaffed projects that, in the end, provided little value or assurance. Although it was an important issue, the Y2K hysteria frustrated many companies and changed their project management culture permanently.

- **The Internet Bubble Burst:** At the same time the Y2K projects were active, the dot-com rush was on. Companies invested billions of dollars into ideas and concepts that were not developed and/or were unsuccessful. The excitement generated by the bubble caused many organizations to forego their normal operating procedures and invest with blind faith.

- **Sarbanes-Oxley Act:** The Sarbanes-Oxley Act (SOX) was enacted in 2002 to combat wide corruption into the accounting and auditing practices of North American companies. This legislation was intended to enforce accountability and governance for organizations.

- **IT Governance:** To comply with SOX, many companies started to try to quantify the spending of the IT budget. It became quickly apparent that most organizations did not understand the cost of maintaining the business.

- **Business User Frustration:** The business users of IT have become frustrated with the lack of information for projects and information technology. The IT department often has one of the largest budgets of any organization, yet the accounting of spending is the least available.

The frustration of consumers, the business units, and executives have all created a focus for organizations. The new focus is accountability. The general public, as well as the stockholders, board of directors, and employees, are demanding accountability for corporate spending. This trend is forcing corporations to improve at providing data that they are not used to providing. Project progress is becoming more and more important. Life-cycle costing (the cost of a new product or program throughout its entire life including maintenance and support) is becoming more important. Businesses are quickly trying to implement controls and governance to ensure the accountability.

▪ Strategic Positioning of Project Management

The first major change that the new governance policies were effecting was project progress. Companies needed to know the overall budget for a project and how the project was performing. One of the largest reasons accountability became so important was that by law, an executive could face both civil and criminal charges for inaccurately reporting on the company's performance. Most companies have established support procedures, so many of the larger investments and those that qualified under SOX, were changes or enhancements to the organization. Essentially, they were projects. Now that projects and the accountability of their performance could lead to criminal charges for executives, project management became extremely important.

Many organizations plunged into project management with full force. They began to implement project management offices, hire PMs, and properly train many of their internal resources. This focus on project management can be seen by the sharp increase in both membership and certifications of Project Management Institute®. Organizations needed to know where they were making investments and how the projects were progressing.

As PMs began to provide this information to their respective organizations, another item became clear. Projects only account for 20 percent of an organization's budget. The increased visibility showed how projects were progressing, but it also showed that the organization needed to understand the other 80 percent of the budget. One of the newest terms in business today is *IT Governance*. IT Governance essentially is split into two main areas:

- **Operational Support (80 percent):** IT departments spend up to 80 percent of their budgets maintaining the existing environment and "keeping the lights on." IT Governance means that organizations should actively be monitoring the demand and cost of the existing investments. This will lead to cost reduction strategies and data-based conversations with business units about future growth opportunities.

- **Strategic Growth (20 percent):** If 80 percent of the spending is maintaining the business, then that leaves only 20 percent to invest in the growth of the organization. With so little to invest, it is more important than ever to ensure that the investment balances cost, risk, and value to an organization to make sure that the right projects are completed.

As companies try to establish what is operational support versus strategic growth, they are in need of some key skill sets. Those skill sets include planning, estimating, proactive risk management, communications management, and completion of objectives. They need project management.

▧ What CIOs Need to Know

Chief information officers (CIOs) are being challenged more than ever to quantify their budgets. One chief information officer said that he was frustrated about his ability to establish his needs. His peers will go into a budget meeting and are able to quantify their desires. For example:

- For every 1,000 calls that are received by the call center, another agent is needed to answer the phone.
- For every 500 applications received, a new underwriter is needed to process them.
- For every 1,000 orders received, a new assembly person is required.
- For every 1,000 claims received, a new claims adjuster is needed.

The chief information officer would state that he needs five more developers. When asked why, he could only respond that his department was busy. When they asked what they were busy doing, he couldn't give a quantified answer. Executives are faced with many questions:

- What is the best investment that can be made for the future?
- How can I be sure that the services that are internally delivered are comparable with those provided by external providers—are we competitive?
- How can we deliver a robust and accurate budget?
- How can we be sure we are making the best investment decisions?
- Business users don't understand the real costs of the services they demand. How can we give them the information they need?
- Everyone wants more services. How can we prioritize and choose the services that are best for the company?

These are pressing questions and issues that executives must answer. With the advent of SOX and other controls, executives can ill afford to make poor choices. They need accurate data and solid projections to make key strategic decisions. They need to understand the current environment better to plan for the future. They need the assistance of a PM.

▨ What PMs Need to Provide

PMs are the key strategic resource that can help a company and its executives make great decisions. The concepts presented earlier in this book have all lent themselves to obtaining better and more accurate data on a project-by-project basis. They have also helped establish the resource utilization. It is now time to take all of the collected data and begin to aggregate the data for decision making. The PM will need to provide:

- **List of active projects:** Information from all current active projects will need to be combined. This includes resource utilization, current progress, estimates for the completion of the projects, and the goals or objectives the project supports.
- **List of demand:** A list of future projects with resource estimates, cost estimates, and a forecast detailing the benefits of completing the project will need to be compiled so that decisions can be made as to which ones to pursue.

- **Understanding resource utilization for support and maintenance projects:** The PM must establish a way to capture the true utilization of resources and the demand of the operational support effort.

- **Understanding of the company's direction:** The PM must understand the direction of the company and how each current and potential project fits into that strategy.

- **Resource estimates for demand:** The resource estimates for all potential projects must be estimated to the best level of understanding based on known information. Some projects may not be selected based on resource utilization, so the more accurate the estimate is, the better the utilization of resources will be.

- **Solid project plans with accurate dates:** The current projects must be supported by detailed and accurate project plans and completion dates to accurately forecast what resources will be available to fulfill demand.

The project management office can be tasked with collecting, maintaining, and quantifying the data collected. All of this data will be utilized to support the earlier executive question list. Collection of this data by groups that do not follow the principles of project management will get wildly varying results. Estimates could be widely varied, and decisions may not have strong fact-based data backing them up. Therefore, the PM is now a strategic resource in enabling an organization to provide governance.

Software Assistance with Governance

An interesting transformation has occurred along with the strategic positioning of the PM. Enterprise Project Management (EPM) solutions are transforming into governance solutions. Two of the market leaders in this space, CA's Clarity (formerly Niku) and Microsoft Project have both built governance solutions based on their project management platforms. There was an explosive growth in the utilization of CA Clarity and Microsoft Project after the Year 2000 project. Companies were desperate to gain visibility into project progress. They began to ask for and keep an eye on project plans. The software systems then began to allow the tracking of time, which provided new visibility and new challenges.

Executives wanted 100 percent time tracking for accountability. They needed to quantify where the 80 percent of operational support was being spent. They looked to their EPM solutions, but there was a new quandary. Project management systems were set up for projects. They were not set up to track time against maintenance or operational support, paid time off, holidays, and so forth. There was a huge and sometimes painful gap. The systems were handling time on projects very well, but the other areas were cumbersome to create and maintain. This would lead to poor data and adoption that did not solve the real problem. This issue provided the final push for EPM solutions to provide assistance with governance.

Microsoft Project and CA's Clarity both provided avenues to track time against operational support, other work, as well as application support, and thus, the transformation was complete. The software systems now facilitate the governance of spending and time across the enterprise. PMs can use the systems to set cost plans, prepare a total view of resource utilization, and manage enterprise priorities. As stated earlier, however, it will take the facilitation of project management and project management techniques to truly garner the information necessary to provide governance to organizations.

The Proactive Approach

PMs can now employ a more proactive approach to applying governance to an organization. The first main objective is to collect all current initiatives and ensure that the data is quantified and qualified. It must be a comprehensive view of all initiatives, including active projects, demand for projects, operational support, maintenance, and any other activities that constitute the time and focus from resources.

The next step in the proactive approach includes collecting and assessing all of the risks to current initiatives. This will ensure that governance is adhering to regulatory compliance as well as providing all of the data necessary to make key decisions. The focus of governance is to ensure that the organization is working on the right items to maximize value and mitigate risk to the organization. Some projects may be cancelled or stopped "midflight" should a major risk be uncovered or if the project does not support a strategic objective of the company. There are many companies that will find out months or even years later that significant costs and time were spent on projects that did not bring value to the enterprise. Collecting the risk and value data of all current projects will help align the current investments with the organization's goals. Those that match continue; those that do not are stopped, and new projects are selected that are more closely aligned to the organization's objectives.

The third step in the proactive approach is to create metrics and measurements for all relevant data on initiatives. This will help measure the progress and success of the current initiatives and help identify areas of improvement. Project Management Institute® teaches that all metrics should be defined in the planning phase of a project. Governance will standardize those metrics so that they are a true comparison. The advent of business intelligence and dashboarding technology has created fantastic avenues to record and display this information. The key is to identify and measure metrics that will assist in finding problems early. Two of the metrics that are well known but not used as often come from the Earned Value management. Those metrics are Cost Performance Index (CPI) and Schedule Performance Index (SPI).

CPI is a measurement of the planned cost of a project in relation to the actual cost and is represented by a number such as 0.7 or 1.2. It is read as "for every dollar that I am spending, I am getting (CPI) in return." If your CPI is 1.2, then you are ahead of budget (tracking at 1.20 worth of value for every dollar spent). SPI shows how the schedule is progressing and is tracked as a similar number to CPI. It is read as "the team is operating at (SPI) percent efficiency." If your SPI is below a 1.0, you are behind schedule. If it is above a 1.0, you are ahead of schedule. Earned value is a popular concept because it can whittle down the entire project to two simple numbers. The numbers will tell you if the project is ahead or behind schedule as well as over or under budget. The reason many organizations do not employ earned value is that it requires time tracking to the task level. To be successful, the PM must know the original estimate for the task, the time spent on the task, and the amount of work accomplished on the task. For many organizations, it is difficult to get each and every resource to tell the PM the exact time they spent on each task on a project plan. With governance requirements, however, the technology advancements in project management software and the focus from executives earned value, and other measurement techniques are finally getting the support needed to be successful. The PM should define and measure the metrics of each initiative to accurately report progress.

The final step in the proactive process is to standardize all demand to a single point of standardization. Many organizations lose a tremendous amount of money by duplicating initiatives. Until governance, many organizations did not have complete visibility into all current objectives. They normally allowed individual departments to select and complete projects as their needs warranted. There are several PMs out there that have experienced the frustration of implementing a project only to find another department has started an initiative to duplicate the work. One popular soft drink maker saw this within their organization and applied governance methodologies to assist. They have estimated savings in the millions of dollars by applying governance to their new product development. When they want to create a new flavor, they used to assign a team and begin work. Later, they would find out that another country had unsuccessfully tried that flavor before. To combat this problem, they placed a governance model that would become a single point of demand to ensure that the idea was truly new, that it was viable, and that it supported the company's objectives. Implementing these steps has stopped duplication of failed projects, created a more streamlined and controlled process, and has increased productivity levels by ensuring that the work completed is the right work for the company.

There are several organizations that want a quick fix, a software package, or to flip a switch and have governance. The reality is that it is an involved process that will take time to develop and implement. The encouraging part is that the steps to a proactive approach to governance are nothing new for PMs. The PM is now a strategic resource that is desperately needed to ensure the success of the new governance models in modern-day organizations.

MAKING POSITIVE
CHANGE TO YOUR
CORPORATE CULTURE

W e've talked about various aspects of project management throughout this book. Your success as a project manager (PM) does not rest entirely on you and your team, however. Corporate culture can make or break project management. Despite this, great project management can and will have a positive impact on the corporate culture. Creating an open and honest atmosphere and having solid data to rely on will begin to affect and change the conversations within the organization.

■ How Corporate Culture Affects Project Management

Corporate culture can make project management very difficult. The downfall of many organizations is how they manage change. Change is normally a mandated event for reasons unknown. Whether it is a new strategy, the latest technology, or a shift in priorities, project management is generally the last to find out. In many corporate cultures, the company has decided that a change or a project will be completed, developed high-level estimates, or selected an end date before they even talk to a PM. Take a look at the following example.

A chief executive officer (CEO) went to a software convention and saw the latest and greatest software to automate his business processes. He immediately made the decision that he wanted it. He asked the vendor how long it should take to get the system up and running, and the answer was 4 months. The CEO then returned to his company and demanded the new system be up and operational in 4 months. Nobody challenged the demand, so a project was opened and a mandated date was set. Bill was the PM.

The vendor obviously doesn't know how long it would take the CEO's organization to install the software and couldn't possibly know the complexities of the organization. Therefore, it is likely that it will take longer than 4 months to complete the task. Afraid to present this information to the CEO, the project team feverishly tries to complete the implementation on time and begins to degrade the quality and not test as intently to save time. The end result is an overdue project that does not meet the CEO's satisfaction. The CEO is then frustrated at the project management process and implements controls to stop project failure from happening again. The controls often further limit Bill's ability or further delay implementation of projects. The result is an endless cycle of misunderstandings that leads to more corporate bureaucracy. The bureaucracy begins to stack up to the point where there is more time spent dealing with forms, approvals, and meaningless activities than actually planning and properly executing a project.

Here is another great example of how bureaucracy can stack up on a company. A new PM, Randall, went to work for a large organization. When he asked for a project process for how to move a technology project through the IT organization, he found that one did not exist. He then worked with his IT liaisons to put together a typical project plan for the organization. Each area of IT had its own forms, idiosyncrasies, and service level agreements. For example, the server team would need 10 days to build a server from the time that it arrived. They would also need 5 days' advance notice to schedule the server build. In putting together the service level agreements and the process, Randall found that it would take a minimum of 6 months to navigate through the technology process to install new technology in the organization. This time frame did not include the actual installation, configuration, or testing of the technology. This amount of time only included the bureaucracy of getting the approvals and framework for the technology. As he dug further into the process, Randall found the following:

- **Technical Design Meetings:** The organization had been burned on several occasions by (1) not understanding the architecture or (2) the vendor not revealing all of the potential issues the new technology would bring. Therefore, the organization put together a team of core IT resources to meet with the vendor, review the technology, and put together a technical design that met security, information integrity, network, scalability, and availability needs. Although this was a fantastic idea that provided great benefit to the organization, the teams (as most IT departments are) were heavily overutilized. It was nearly impossible to schedule the resources at a common time. To combat this, the organization decided to pick a specific time and make sure that the team members blocked off the same day and time each week for these meetings. Another great idea. If there were three projects waiting, however, it could be 3 weeks before the project could get going. There were also times when team members were sick or all issues weren't resolved in the first meeting. In those cases, the project would simply wait for the next available slot. The problem is that every project inevitably becomes delayed because it is waiting for the next slot. In a world where first to market can drive market share, this can become a distinct disadvantage. The key metric to investigate is how much time, money, or market share was lost versus the cost of the project failures. Which one costs more? Most likely, it would be the cost of the technical design.

- **Security Scans:** Some projects caused security breaches and information integrity loss, which is also a huge regulatory concern for organizations. This organization could not ascertain whether the issue was caused by installing the operating system, installing the vendor software, or testing the vendor software. Therefore, they instituted a security scan system that would scan after the initial load, scan after the vendor loaded the software, and scan after testing was complete and before the move to production. Each scan budgeted 10 days, so 30 business days were spent scanning for potential issues.

- **Design Committees:** Due to another type of technology failure, the organization would require any new environment change to go before a committee to discuss the potential issues the technology could bring. Another fantastic idea. The project would have to wait for the committee to meet before it could go forward, however.

Each step was instituted because of a project failure occurring causing pain or a substantial loss to the organization. Each step added was a fantastic idea, but there was never a re-evaluation of each step to ensure that it was delivering the intended value. For example, the security scan process was a valuable step, but 30 days was a bit too much time for the process. It would be nice to find out what caused a portion of the technology to be exposed to a security risk such as the installation of the vendor software or the testing, but in the end, it doesn't matter what caused it, just that it was found and rectified before going into production. Therefore, after further review, the company decided to go to one security scan right before the move to production. This step shaved 20 days or a business month off of the project process.

Putting in checks and balances is a great activity and one that merits action. The issue is that organizations rarely look at the impact the new controls can have on an organization. After publishing the project plan showing 6 months as the process, the organization used in the example revisited many steps and revised the process to make it timelier. There was nothing that was right or wrong in the process. Each step had significance and was designed to keep the same mistakes from occurring again.

Another example is Rashad, a PM who went to work for a large software developer. Rashad was given a list of internal reports and systems that he had to fill out each week. As he looked at all of the systems, he found that many of them were repeating the same information over and over. He wanted to see the value of the information and the controls in place. He decided that for the first 3 weeks, he would fill out the core reports and ensure that he had the information for all of the reports but would only complete the core reports. After 3 weeks, nobody ever asked him for the reports that he did not fill out. Rashad worked for the organization for 6 months and never filled out those reports. He was even audited on his projects for documentation and received a 100 percent passing score. Upon further investigation, every time a major project failure occurred, the organization instituted another report that was to be an early warning sign of potential failure. The problem was that there were so many reports, people forgot which ones were important and which ones were not. Rashad wasn't intentionally not completing his job; he had all of the information. He just was trying to understand the reasoning behind inputting the same information in different formats. He wanted to make sure that he was managing the project, not the project documentation. In the end, nobody ever questioned as to why he didn't fill out all of the reports.

Another organization was using an outsourced system from a vendor. They frequently complained about the expense and lack of response they received from the vendor. A new PM, Robin, was assigned a very simple project that was estimated at less than 1 week's worth of effort. When she received the quote from the vendor, she was utterly shocked. The vendor had estimated the work to take 6 months and cost $30,000. Robin asked for a breakdown of how the estimate was completed and what constituted the $30,000. The vendor replied, "We normally do not share that information with our clients." Robin was outraged. The vendor could charge extraneous costs and not have to support them? When Robin said that 6 months was too long, the vendor stated that they could accelerate the process for an extra $20,000 and it could be completed in 6 weeks. Robin took the information to the project sponsor and fully expected a round of harsh negotiations with the vendor. Instead, the sponsor said, "They do that often to us, but just pay them what they are asking." Robin urged for a negotiation. The sponsor said, "There is nothing we can really do about it. They are our vendor."

These are all examples of how corporate culture can affect project management. The key to each of the examples is that the company was trying to correct the physical issue that caused the project to fail and implemented a specific control to fix it. The organizations didn't look at the overall process and how to improve the management of the project. Each organization tried to put a control in to fix a symptom of the project. The result was bureaucracy on top of bureaucracy.

■ Understanding and Analyzing Corporate Culture

Corporate culture is a difficult aspect to understand and analyze. It takes time, an open mind, and observation to determine the corporate culture of an organization. Even items that appear clear are not very clear. For example, PM Bruce was working on a large initiative with a global organization. In a meeting where the sponsor was not present, the team was discussing whether or not a piece of functionality was included in the scope of the project. Bruce, a consultant, stated that it was a part of the project, while the project team (employees of the customer's organization) said that it was not. Bruce sought out the sponsor to gain clarification. The sponsor agreed with him. Bruce asked the sponsor to state that in the next team meeting. The sponsor agreed. At the next team meeting, the following conversation ensued:

SPONSOR (SPN): "Is there anything else to discuss?"

BRUCE (PM): "Yes. You were going to mention something about the scope."

SPN: "I don't have anything about the scope of the project."

PM: "You know, whether or not to include the functionality."

SPN: "Yes, that functionality should be in the project. Why do you bring it up?"

PM: "Because the team thinks it isn't."

SPN: "Look, as the PM, if you don't know what is in scope and not in scope, then you need to rethink your position."

PM: "I know what's in the scope. I'm referring to the project team. They said it isn't in scope, and you and I discussed this in your office the other day."

SPN: "Don't be smart with me. If you can't communicate to the project team, don't blame it on them."

PM: "I'm not blaming anyone. I'm reminding you of the conversation in your office about whether or not this piece is considered in the scope of the project."

SPN: "I believe I have answered that. This meeting is adjourned."

Bruce was in disbelief. It seemed that the sponsor had forgotten the conversation and also became adversarial about her position. The sponsor then called Bruce's organization and complained about the incident, and Bruce was asked to apologize to the sponsor. He did, however, he still felt like he did nothing wrong. He did do one thing wrong—he failed to recognize the culture of the organization. After the meeting, one of the team members went up to him and said, "Now you know what we go through when dealing with her." Bruce looked back upon the incident later. He realized a few things that he did not see before:

- The only person that really talked throughout the meeting was the sponsor. She was autocratic and authoritarian.
- Anyone who asked questions was quickly shut down, and no other opinions were sought.
- Most of the team was not engaged in the meeting.
- Almost all conversations were very direct and to the point.

After reflection, Bruce realized where he had gone wrong. First, he should have just asked the question of whether the functionality was in scope or not. Instead, he went about in a roundabout fashion instead of asking directly. Second, his approach was trying to make the sponsor say something that she viewed as a challenge to her authority. The third mistake, and most egregious, was continuing the conversation once the initial answer was given. When the sponsor said that the functionality was part of the scope, she then asked why Bruce brought it up. The correct reply would have been, "I was just making sure that I understood properly," and cut off the conversation. Instead, he said that the team did not understand, to which the sponsor took offense. She took offense because Bruce's reply made it seem as if he were stating that she did not communicate properly with her team. It was one misunderstanding after another, however, this kind of situation can be avoided. Although all corporate cultures are unique, there are some steps to properly analyze and observe a corporate culture. Some key observations are:

Observation: In meetings, watch the people who are not talking. What are they doing? Are the engaged? Are they doodling? What is their reaction to the conversations that are occurring?

Outcome: If the entire team is bored or is not engaged, most likely, it is an autocratic or authoritarian culture. The team does not feel that their input is necessary or that their opinion counts.

Observation: When a question is asked in meetings, is the answer a collaborative response, or does the team look to a specific individual and wait for a response from him or her?

Outcome: The person that the team looks to is usually the one in charge and again, is a High "D" personality or autocratic. If there is healthy discussion about the question, then the team is more of a collaborative team.

Observation: A more subtle observation is who will take the head of the table in a meeting. Who is sitting on the right side of the boss?

Outcome: This is more of a subtle observation, and there are many variables such as was the head of the table the only seat open, or were there others available? As a rule, the head of the table is reserved for the sponsor or the senior manager. If someone comes in early to the meeting and takes the head of the table when other seats are available, that person usually is aspiring for that position. The person who chooses to sit on the right side of the senior manager is someone who has aspirations of moving up the corporate ladder. This is not a rule but a guideline.

Observation: Suggest a new technique in a team meeting to accomplish a common task. For example, ask to have the entire team put together a network diagram to plan the project schedule.

Outcome: Was the suggestion quickly met with, "We don't do that here," or, "That won't work here"? Did the team embrace the idea? This observation can show the organization's willingness to embrace change.

There are many other observations that can be made. The key is to make sure that there is an active effort to understand and observe the culture.

◼ What to Do When You Can't Change or Affect Corporate Culture

Of course, there are times when the PM is unable to change or affect the corporate culture. He or she may have tried many different techniques and many different options to introduce change that were all swept away by the corporate culture. It doesn't matter what is suggested, the company refuses to embrace any kind of change. This situation creates a difficult, yet clear decision. If this is the case, can you survive in the current culture? If the culture is stifling your creativity or is a constant source of stress, then the decision is whether or not you are a good fit in that organization. Company cultures are what they are. Each type can attract and retain employees. If you find yourself in one that is unwilling to change or evolve and if it is detrimental to your career path, then it is time to look for a new organization.

If working for a new organization is not the answer, then stick to your guiding principles. Work within the existing culture while maintaining your personal integrity. For example, Devin was the PM hired to build a project management office (PMO) at an organization. The IT department already had a PMO that was separate from the one he was asked to build. There were also two other PMOs in the organization focused on different areas of the business. Devin would have to work very closely with the IT PMO to complete projects. Therefore, he wanted to make sure that they worked very well together. He took the time to meet with the IT PMO, understand their policies, and understand the environment. He realized that the way the IT PMO completed a project was not in alignment with the way that he would prefer to run projects. After meeting with the IT PMO, he met with the people at the other PMOs. The staff at the other PMOs told Devin how the IT PMO did not follow proper project management principles and how they had tried to create policies and procedures to do things the way they thought they should be done, but the IT PMO was reluctant. Devin realized quickly that the IT PMO was the PMO that held the most power and they also owned the most political capital. The other PMOs were viewed as renegade departments trying to do things their way. Devin then made the decision to strictly follow the guidelines of the IT PMO, but he would gather the information and track projects according to his principles. He would have his team run the projects according to his principles and report all of the information and complete the steps in the order that the IT PMO requested. Little by little, and in a nonthreatening way, he would begin to introduce new concepts to the IT PMO. He would not be forceful or even say, "This is the way it is supposed to be done." As his group grew and matured, the IT PMO started to notice the process that the PM was instituting. They started to ask how he knew certain information or would comment on a report that they liked. After some trust was attained, they started to ask Devin his opinion on the process and started to adapt the IT PMO to be more like his. The engaging part was not that portion but rather the overall process. Although it seemed like the IT PMO was morphing to his style, in reality, the IT PMO and his PMs in his PMO started to create their own culture. It involved into a relationship, and trust was being built between the organizations. In the end, the two groups worked together quite successfully, which is what the other PMOs had strived for. The difference was in the approach. To institute change, it is important to first understand the current culture and then begin to assimilate to that culture as the culture begins to assimilate to you. The result is a cohesive whole that institutes change for the better.

Understanding the current culture and why it exists is important for understanding which direction the culture can evolve. Corporate cultures are like a living tree. There is a core that is planted in the ground. Each year, the tree grows by adding mass around the core. A corporate culture can grow the same way. There is a general core that establishes the culture. Each year, the company will grow or there is some attrition. This change leads to a new group that will slowly be wrapped around the core and brought into the culture. To truly analyze and observe the culture, you must find the core.

How to Obtain Executive Sponsorship

Executive sponsorship is one of the most crucial aspects of successful project management; however, many PMs suffer through projects without obtaining the sponsorship they need. For the most part, it is a simple process to obtain the proper sponsorship. Ask! For example, Marge was a consultant who went to meet with an organization to help improve their prioritization process for fixing defects in products. One manager stated that he could never get upper management to assist in prioritizing the requested fixes. He had a limited staff and could only complete a limited amount of fixes per week. Marge asked if the manager had ever asked her own manager specifically to prioritize the work. The manager said that she had not. Marge then went back to the office and asked the upper manager to prioritize the work. The upper manager asked why it was necessary. Marge said that only so much work could be completed

each week, which would leave some items incomplete until the following week. The upper manager then prioritized the work.

Corporate culture sometimes makes employees afraid to ask their bosses for assistance; however, their bosses are exactly who they should go to for assistance. Whether it is fear of repercussions, fear of looking inadequate, or plain fear of approaching a manager, employees tend to resist asking for help. In another example, Jed was a new PM assigned to a PMO. The PMO manager would continually assign Jed work. He often felt overwhelmed and was working nights and weekends to keep up with all of his commitments. Finally, after almost a year of working at that pace, Jed became frustrated and approached his boss. He stated that he felt overworked and was tired of being overcommitted. The PMO manager was surprised. He said, "All you have to do is say that you are at capacity, and I will find someone else to do the work. If you keep saying yes when I ask, I assume you have the capacity." Jed assumed that the PMO manager was aware of all of the commitments. Although it was a simple miscommunication, it caused great and unnecessary strain on Jed. If he had asked for prioritization or announced his concern about being overburdened the first time it occurred, he could have found out then.

Getting the proper executive sponsorship is a matter of communicating properly. Ask for what is needed and be prepared to back up the request. Believe it or not, upper managers are not evil people consistently conspiring to keep the workers down. They have tough decisions and have a workload to manage as well. Having the facts, research, and options formulated and presented to the sponsor will aide in getting the sponsorship you desire. For example:

BAD CONVERSATION: "I am overloaded and can't do everything! Can't you give something to someone else?"

GOOD CONVERSATION: "I can complete eight of the 12 items on my task list. Which eight are most important?"

BAD CONVERSATION: "I need a risk contingency reserve of 10 percent of the budget."

GOOD CONVERSATION: "I need $5,000 of risk contingency reserve to properly account for this risk register and potential outcomes."

BAD CONVERSATION: "There is no way to make the date you requested."

GOOD CONVERSATION: "In order to meet the date requested, I need some assistance. Looking at the plan, we could increase resources on this task, but it could cost a bit more than we anticipated. We could, however, remove this requirement and still come in on time. Which would you like to do?"

Most managers who complain that they do not have appropriate sponsorship are usually not giving the sponsors what they need to make a decision. If sponsorship is needed, formulate the question or issue that requires a response, provide the data that is necessary to make a proper decision, and ask the sponsor. It is amazing how many projects fail or issues that are created by the mere fact that the PM assumes that the sponsor is aware of the issues.

What to Do When Executive Sponsorship Is Not as You Hoped

There are times that sponsorship is not going to be as you hoped. The only thing to do in that situation is to keep fantastic documentation. Still follow the process written previously mentioned, but document all requests for action or decision and the results of the action. It can be a very frustrating situation for a PM. There is no easy way to resolve the issue.

It is possible to seek another sponsor. Depending on the organization, if the sponsor is at a certain level, it may be possible to seek the sponsor's manager for assistance. Ken is a PM who relayed a story of when a project was being derailed by the sponsor. Every time he asked for a decision, it was stalled or never answered. Phone calls and e-mails were not returned. He was forced with a tough decision: continue to fail on the project that could cost him his job or go over the sponsor's head, which could cost him his job. In the end, he decided to go over the sponsor's head. When an investigation ensued, Ken was able to document the requests for the decisions and show the number of calls and e-mails ignored. The sponsor was eventually replaced, but it is not that easy for many PMs. If the sponsorship is not as you expect, first ensure that you are communicating properly with the sponsor. If the sponsorship is still not as requested, then it may be time to look higher in the organization.

Another more disheartening story happened to Amanda, a new senior PM at an organization. She was hired to bring in new project management techniques and help mature the organization's project

management practices. She was hired into the PMO of the organization and reported to the PMO manager. One of her first projects was to integrate the accounting departments of two separate entities. The project team met and pulled together a scope of work for the project. The key dates were:

- Hire new employees by the end of the second quarter.
- Have new employees shadow the employees of the other organization to understand their policies and procedures. Have all processes documented by the end of the third quarter.
- Analyze the gaps in the processes and create new processes. The two organizations would close the books in parallel and then analyze to see whether they arrived at the same numbers. This step was to be complete by the end of the fourth quarter.
- The new organization would complete the closing of the books while being shadowed by the old organization. All accounting operations would be transferred by the end of the first quarter of the next year.

The project was aggressive and risky. Additionally, if the numbers were not calculated properly, it could result in a regulatory fine and presented a reputation risk. Ken created an in-depth project charter complete with deliverables, risks, assumptions, constraints, and key enablers for success. The last page of the charter was a signature page calling for the signature of all of the principals involved including the project sponsor who was the chief financial officer (CFO). Ken presented the charter to the PMO manager for approval. The PMO manager stated that although there is value in the charter, they really didn't do that level of detail in that area. Culturally, they normally do not ask for signatures on project objectives. Instead, they produce a one- to two-page bullet point list and send that to all team members. Ken protested and stated that because it was such a risky and strategic project, he would like to try to have the document signed. The PMO manager refused again. Ken was relegated to producing the bullet point list.

A few months later, the project was behind schedule. They were nearing the end of the third quarter and had not fully staffed the teams, which was due by the end of the second quarter. The organization had to spend money on consultants to document the policies and procedures of the other organization to ensure that the project did not fall too far behind. For the first time in months, the CFO attended the project status meeting. In the meeting, the following conversation occurred:

CFO: "How is the project progressing?"

KEN (PM): "Right now, we are quite behind and over budget. We haven't staffed the department as we had hoped. Therefore we're using consultants to do the documentation. That's fine, but it creates a new risk that the new employees will not be able to become familiar with the processes in time for the parallel close in the fourth quarter."

CFO: "Parallel close? We are supposed to be fully cut over by the end of the year."

PM: "The schedule we have produced says that cutover is at the end of the first quarter."

CFO: "I don't know who approved that. It's always been the end of the year."

PM: "Did you get the project charter?"

CFO: "If I did, I obviously didn't understand or would have agreed to the date being the end of the first quarter. We have to accelerate this project."

Unfortunately, Ken really did not have a leg to stand on in the negotiations with the CFO. The other issue was that the CFO did not approve additional expenses to try to accelerate the schedule. The key point of the story is that had the PMO manager allowed the document to be signed, one of two outcomes would have occurred. The first would have been a scope change to the document accounting for the new demands. The project would still be accelerated, but at least Ken could have pointed out the signature and had more negotiation room with the CFO. The second outcome could have been a re-write of the charter. If the date was always the end of the year, the CFO would have caught it and asked for it to be fixed before signing.

The next question people generally ask is, what should the senior PM have done? This is a difficult choice. When executive sponsorship is not as you hoped, there are really only two decisions. The first is to understand what you have to work with and do your best. This is not an exciting or breakthrough concept. At least you understand what it is going to be like and you understand the additional items you may have to complete to deal with the situation. The other decision is to leave the company. That is a harder choice for many individuals but is sometimes the right choice. In the end, the senior PM felt that he would not be successful in that type of environment and chose to leave the company.

How to Get Your Sponsor Motivated and Interested in Your Project

Motivating sponsors is one of the easier topics for corporate culture. Sponsors are motivated by successful results. A true definition of a sponsor is the one who financially enables the project. This means there could be a fair amount of risk in initially deciding to do the project. The PM is responsible for delivering the expected result on time and on budget. Delivering that success can be the greatest motivator.

To keep the sponsor interested, make sure that the appropriate communications are sent to him or her in a timely manner. The earlier a deviation from the plan is recognized, the more options the sponsor has to rectify without impact on the project. For example, if a project plan is not being monitored and controlled properly, then it will be near the end of the project before it will be discovered that the plan is off track. This limits the actions that can be taken to remedy the deviation before it affects the completion criteria of the project. Most projects will have quality covertly degraded when nearing the end of the task and when the end date is in jeopardy. With proper project management, as discussed throughout this book, deviations are found early and presented immediately. This strategy allows the sponsor more time to decide what the impact could be. For instance, if the job was a development project and the design phase finished 3 weeks late, the plan that is not being monitored and controlled would not see the impact of the 3-week deviation until the completion date nears. At that time, the development is most likely completed, and the only activity that can be shortened is the testing time before moving a product into production. A plan that is being updated properly would have foreseen the impact of the 3-week delay before development even began. This advance notice would allow the sponsor to choose to try to accelerate the development, remove a requirement, or extend the date. The difference between these two scenarios is that the earlier the deviation is found, the more options there are to resolve the plan. Bringing information of this nature to the sponsor's attention in a timely fashion will keep him or her interested.

Another issue that PMs tend to forget is that the sponsor is part of the team who should be recognized and rewarded as well. So many projects and PMs focus on creating a reward and recognition system for the project team, that they forget to include the sponsors in that plan. Sponsors are people too, and they like to be recognized and rewarded for their efforts as much as the team. Keep them in mind during those times, keep them well informed, and ask for their assistance. Performing these steps can lead to the engaged, interested sponsor that you deserve!

CONCLUSION

This book is a chapter-by-chapter road map to improving project management skills and resolving common project issues. The destination is great project management. The collection of these theories, ideas, and systems offers true project management strategy. The systems discussed throughout the book are based on real and practical solutions from real projects. They are not just theories or ideas but rather a proven formula for success in setting and meeting the context of a project. These systems do work. They bring positive change to the organizations from the ground up, but they are not an overnight solution. It takes time, effort, and often courage to affect positive change in a corporation. Applying these theories and systems will also take time, effort, and courage.

Frank was a consultant hired by an organization to come in and help with project management. The company was tired of projects consistently failing and wanted someone to assess their process and recommend changes to help them forecast and meet their project objectives.

Frank spent some time completing the assessment and scheduled a meeting to reveal the results and suggest the first steps. After his first suggestion, the project sponsor (who was also the chief information officer of the organization) said, "That's not how we do it here. That's not going to work." This was also the chief information officer's response to the subsequent suggestions. Frank politely ended the engagement. If the company is not willing to change their process or look at other ideas, they are not ready to change. You, as the reader, must make a key decision: Are you willing to change how you manage projects? If the answer is yes, then start with the concepts in this book, as they will work if applied properly. Even if your organization does not support change, you can still improve how you estimate, bring issues to your project teams, turn projects around, and give great, unemotional, and trustworthy information. If your answer is no, then many of these systems simply will not work. *Project Management That Works* can lead you to more successful project management and help understand where the gaps are in project philosophy. *Project Management That Works* gives you the tips, tools, and techniques to make your project a success!

GLOSSARY

Assumption: Any presumption made during the planning process. When creating project plans, there are many guesses and interpretations. Any of these interpretations should be a documented as assumptions.

Baseline: A line in the sand. A baseline is what is used to compare actual project performance of cost, time, and requirements to the planned cost, time, and requirements.

Client: The person(s), group, or company for whom the project is undertaken.

Cost Performance Index: A statistical measurement of project costs to establish if the project is under or over budget. The resulting measurement is a number such as 1.3 or .3. The interpretation of this index is anything over a 1.0 is ahead of budget and anything underneath 1.0 is behind budget.

Critical Path: The longest path through the network diagram which represents the shortest amount of time in which a project can be completed. If a task is on the critical path, any movement of dates (completion early or late) will affect the overall project completion date.

8/80 Hour Rule: A rule of thumb for breaking down deliverables into appropriate work packages. If a work package can be reasonably estimated between 8 and 80 hours, then no further decomposition is required.

Enterprise Project Management: The methodology of managing projects for an entire organization.

Dashboard: A collection of metrics and measurements showing quickly the overall health of a project or collection of projects.

Defect: An impactful event, imperfection, or shortcoming to the end customer. If the customer experiences an unexpected event during the consumption of goods, it is known as a defect.

Deliverables: A quantifiable task or good that is to be developed by the project.

Done: Do not look here for the definition of done. Read Chapter 5!

Feedback Loop: An active listening practice to ensure that the receiver has understood the sender's message.

Groupthink: A phenomenon that causes one individual or the minority of the group to not speak up or share information with the majority of the group because of either fear or apathy.

Historical Information: Project artifacts that can be referenced during the planning of a new project. These artifacts include project schedules, issue logs, risk logs, project charters, and any other documentation created by a previous project.

Iron Triangle: The early definition of the Iron Triangle or Triple Constraint was cost, schedule, and quality. It has since added customer satisfaction and scope of work. The Iron Triangle is an illustration to show the impact of changing one of the key areas of the project on the other key areas of the project.

Issue: Something that causes a deviation on one of the plans of the project.

Lessons Learned: A documentation of key events on a project and how to avoid issues or enhance opportunities on future projects.

Life Cycle Costing: A technique that looks at the overall cost of a project including maintenance, support, and upgrades for a defined length of time such as 5 years.

Mandated Date: An imposed date placed on the project. These can be caused by regulatory or legal requirements, business needs, or external pressure from a variety of sources.

Network Diagram: A graphical representation of the project work packages arranged from start to finish showing dependencies between tasks.

Open Workbench: A tool written by Niku that is an open source application that competes with Microsoft Project. This application can be downloaded from http://www.openworkbench.org.

Padding: The practice of arbitrarily adding time to a project to account for risk or poor estimates. Padding is not an acceptable practice in project management since it is not based on risk or contingencies.

Passive Acceptance: The act of assuming an answer or completion based on a one-way communication. For example, an email that states "If I don't hear back by Friday, I will assume this task is complete."

PERT: A statistical formula utilizing three point estimates to estimate the unknown. (Best Case + (4*Most Likely) + Worst Case)/6

Project Charter: A document that formally recognizes the project and grants the project manager their authority to run the project.

Project Plan: More than just a schedule. A project plan consists of a schedule, resource plan, procurement plan, issue and risk plan, quality plan, cost plan, scope management plan, change management plan, and any other appropriate plans needed to govern the project.

Project Schedule: A list of tasks needed to complete the project showing start dates, finish dates, resources, and predecessors.

Quality: The definition of quality for project management is the degree in which the scope of the project will be completed.

Quality Plan: This plan ensures that the scope of the project is delivered to the expectations of the stakeholders within the range decided by the project team.

Response Plan: A planned response to identified risks.

Resource: A person, company, group, material, or anything that is utilized in the completion of a project.

Risk: A positive or negative occurrence that could potentially cause a deviation to any of the project plans.

Sarbanes Oxley Act: Legislation that is a result of many of the American corporate scandals in the early 2000s. This act has placed more pressure on the accuracy of financial statements issues by companies and has had a profound impact on many organizations' project management methodologies.

Schedule Performance Index: A statistical measurement of a project schedule to establish if the project is under or over schedule. The resulting measurement is a number such as 1.3 or .3. The interpretation of this index is that anything over a 1.0 is ahead of schedule and anything underneath 1.0 is behind schedule.

Scope: The definition of what is and what is not a part of the project.

Sponsor: The sponsor is the person or persons ultimately responsible for the project. Sponsors also generally provide the financial backing to complete the project.

Status Report: A report given on a regular basis to show the progress of the project that is the primary communication tool to the entire project team including stakeholders.

Triple Constraint: see Iron Triangle.

Work Breakdown Structure: A graphical hierarchy of all the work needed to complete the project. This is completed from a top-down approach and it contains all of the deliverables needed to complete the project.

Work Package: The lowest level necessary to complete a work breakdown structure. A work package can be a single task or group of tasks that fit within the 8/80 hour rule.

INDEX

ABOUT THE AUTHORS

Rick A. Morris, PMP, is an ITIL Practitioner, consultant, author, mentor, and creator of a nonprofit foundation to promote Project Management in charities and other nonprofits. Rick is an accomplished project manager and public speaker. His appetite for knowledge and passion for the profession makes him a sought-after speaker at PMI chapters and various civic organizations and a frequent guest lecturer at local universities. He holds the PMP (Project Management Professional), MPM (Masters of Project Management), Six Sigma Green Belt, MCTS, MCSE, TQM, ATM-S, ITIL, and ISO certifications. Rick has worked for organizations such as GE, Xerox, and CA and has consulted to numerous clients in a wide variety of industries including financial services, entertainment, construction, nonprofit, hospitality, pharmaceutical, retail, and manufacturing. Currently, Rick is the Chief Operating Officer for Highmark Technology. An active member of the Project Management Institute and currently the President of the Birmingham Chapter, Rick is no stranger to being center stage in front of large groups of people. At the early age of 11, Rick was a Walt Disney World Performer in its seasonal shows. In high school, he worked at MGM Studios on various projects including the New Mickey Mouse Club. Taking the experience of his youth and blending it with the knowledge he attained throughout his career, Rick has been able to inspire and mentor many project managers. His blend of real-world experience and down-to-earth delivery style makes his passion for the profession contagious.

Brette McWhorter Sember has a B.A. and J.D. and is an attorney and mediator. She is the author of over 30 books, including *The Essential Supervisor's Handbook* (Career Press) and *Managing Bad Apples* (Adams Media). Her other titles include *The Complete Credit Repair Kit* (Sourcebooks), *The Divorce Organizer & Planner* (McGraw-Hill), *Unmarried with Children* (Adams Media), and many more. Her website is http://www.BretteSember.com.